VFX and CG Survival Guide for Filmmakers

VFX and CG Survival Guide for Producers
By Farhan Qureshi
Published: January 2013
Publisher: Digitopia Studios Ltd
All rights reserved

www.digitopiafilm.com

No part of this publication may be reproduced, stored in retrieval system, copied in any form or by any means, electronic, mechanical, photocopying, recorded or otherwise transmitted without written permission from the publisher. You must not circulate this book in any format.

Book Reviews

From Amazon.com
http://www.amazon.com/kindle/dp/B00BDV8GY2/

5.0 out of 5 stars **Essential Reading for VFX Producers** February 12, 2013
By Richard Klein

In this well-written and clever book Qureshi uses his experience as an accomplished VFX artist to shine a light on one of the Visual Effects industry's weakest spots: VFX management/production. His Survival Guide clarifies Producers, Directors and all other people involved in the production of computer generated images on a crucial item: the pipeline seen from the perspective of the artist. This book gives them and aspiring artists a deep understanding of all the steps it takes to make a VFX scene "on the floor" and, most importantly, how they could and should intervene to make the process flow in a more effective way. This unique work covers an important gap in the industry and would definitely help most workplaces where I, as a professional CG artist, have passed through. A definite "must read".

5.0 out of 5 stars **Great advice for producers** March 20, 2013
By jamesm
Amazon Verified Purchase

The VFX and CG survival guide is a very useful book. If you are a film maker who wants to understand how best to plan your VFX workflow this book is invaluable resource. It covers all the main areas which you will need during production. It's written in a very clear and concise way that make the information easy to understand.

VFX and CG Survival Guide for Filmmakers and Producers

There's not really any other resources like this out there, so this book is very helpful for all film makers and producers.

From Amazon.co.uk
www.amazon.co.uk/kindle/dp/B00BDV8GY2/

5.0 out of 5 stars A GEM OF A BOOK! 15 Feb 2013
By DANTE

This book simplified the complex word of VFX and CG and allowed me to grasp the information in a straightforward way. The fact live projects have been used eases the process along considerably.

This book is the first of its kind and in my option is the only book you will need. Coming into the industry with a little knowledge I'm now able to exchange knowledge with the guys who have been in the industry for years. It's a real gem and will save you time and money while furthering your skill set.

5.0 out of 5 stars Real Life Examples 19 Feb 2013
By Mr. M. Kebir
Amazon Verified Purchase

I was looking for a book with real life examples and my research lead me to this book. I am glad I bought it. Well recomended!

5.0 out of 5 stars Excellent and informative 26 Feb 2013
By Clouds
Amazon Verified Purchase

I really enjoyed this book. It's a great read, concise and to the point. No surprise that the artist had to write it and YES all the producers should read it.
Comment |
Was this review helpful to you?

5.0 out of 5 stars **Does what it says on the tin!**, 21 Feb 2013

By
Mr Taylor - See all my reviews

Amazon Verified Purchase(What is this?)

This review is from: VFX and CG Survival Guide for Producers and Film makers (VFX and CG Survival Guides) (Kindle Edition)

Very useful book that will help guide you through the steps of visual effects and computer generated images. Great Buy!

About the Author

Farhan has been working in VFX for over ten years, he has worked across film, TV, games and live events. Farhan has worked on big budget Hollywood movies including Batman Begins, Poseidon, Alien vs Predator, 3 Harry Potter movies and The Chronicles of Riddick. Farhan has worked in AAA games, TV commercials and low/no budget independent movies. Farhan provided fully animated sequences on the London 2012 Olympics graphics, idents, stings and corporate movies.

Companies which Farhan has plied his trade include The Moving Picture Company, Double Negative Visual Effects, Codemasters Software, Aardman Animation, Crystal CG and Mokko Studios. Currently (April 2013) Farhan is working at Microsoft Games (Lionhead) in the UK.

Farhan has produced movies on various budgets, all of which he has managed the special effects and animation and has seen all the projects from concept stage through to post production. Farhan also teaches courses in VFX and CGI. Farhan has worked with many excellent producers whom he has observed and learnt from. In this book Farhan will present real life examples, it is not a theory book but is based on practice that VFX producer will need to know to make effective decisions and avoid pitfalls that needlessly beseech many productions.

Acknowledgments

There are lot of people who have helped me write this book, both directly and indirectly. Directly thanks go to Nathan Eyers, VFX producer who I worked with on many of the London 2012 Olympics projects, for going through, checking and advising me on the book's contents. All the Contributors for their time and allowing me to share their insight and work. To my wife who put up with me writing through the night and then subsequently letting me sleep through the six am nappy changes.

Of course a lot of thanks goes to the producers with whom I have worked with. Both those 'good' producers who have taught me so much and the 'other' for the experiences that have laid out the book's structure and guided me to write exactly what is required to make sure.

About the Contributors

Article Contributions

Foreword and Ten Golden Rules by Nathan Eyers- Nathan Eyers - Producer London 2012 Games'

'Nathan Eyers worked as a Producer on the London 2012 Olympic games, overseeing animations that were played on the BBC, and other major international broadcast stations, as well as live events and online. Nathan has extensive experience managing teams of CG artists in the UK and abroad, delivering projects to clients internationally, and outsourcing with post-production houses.
http://www.linkedin.com/pub/nathan-eyers/17/605/25

Case study 2:
Shotgun and Revolver Streamline Prime Focus' Global VFX Collaboration on Men In Black 3 - Shotgun Software, http://www.shotgunsoftware.com

Image contributions

Cover Design
Rooful Ali, http://www.racreation.com

Concept Art
Vincent Jenkins, http://vincentjenkins.blogspot.co.uk/
Stephen Trumble, http://www.stephentrumble.com/
Kelvin Johnson, http://uk.linkedin.com/pub/kelvin-johnson/32/970/679

Modelling
Ben Godi 2012, www.selwy.com www.ben-godi.com

Digital Matte Painting
Vincent Jenkins, http://vincentjenkins.blogspot.co.uk/

HDRI
Owen Boyer, www.HDRMill.com

Lighting Passes
RockKiss Digital Media Entertainment,
http://www.rockkiss.co.uk

VFX and CG Survival Guide for Filmmakers and Producers

Contents

Book Reviews 3
About the Author 6
Acknowledgments 7
About the Contributors 8
Image contributions 9
Foreword 12
Introduction 13
    Why this book is important 13
    The aim of this book is 16
    Why is there such a problem with producers in the VFX industry?
    16
Part 1 - Producer Essentials 19
    Concept art & story boarding essentials 19
    Previz essentials 23
    Match moving essentials 24
    Approving matchmoves 26
    Modelling essentials 28
    Rigging Essentials 30
    Texturing essentials 32
    Shading Essentials 33
    Animation and motion capture essentials 34
    Digital Matte Painting and HDRI 37
    Effects essentials 39

VFX and CG Survival Guide for Filmmakers and Producers

    Crowd simulation Essentials 44

    Lighting and rendering essentials 48

    Render Farms 52

Part 2: Scheduling - getting shots through the pipeline and understanding dependencies 61

    Case study 1: producing a short CGI film from scratch 61

    Case study 2: Shotgun and Revolver Streamline Prime Focus' Global VFX Collaboration on Men In Black 3 71

    Case Study 3: Integrating CGI and VFX into live action 75

    Case study 4: CG in computer games - adding programmers, designers and QA into the mix 79

Part 3: Producer Practicalities 85

    Weapon of choice - working on multiple software in the same show 85

    Working late nights + weekends != good producer 87

    Worked Example – a bear walks into a bar 90

Part 4: Low/No Budget VFX 93

    Can low/no Budget filmmaking still have VFX? 93

    Plan 93

    Taking a VFX supervisor on set 95

    In post 96

Part 5: Conclusion 99

    How to be a good producer 99

    In closing 111

    The Ten Golden Rules by Nathan Eyers 112

Foreword

"One of the first lessons to learn on the road to becoming a successful producer is to stop, think, and plan your way through the production. Before any of that, read this book. I wish I had."
- Nathan Eyers,   VFX Producer
   http://www.linkedin.com/pub/nathan-eyers/17/605/25

"VFX is more and more becoming a reality when it comes to producing TVCs and Featurefilm.   It is cruicial as a producer to understand the whole process and also being an asset in the postproduction rather than a obstacle"
- Stefan Ström, UtopiaPeople
   http://www.utopiapeople.com

"As visual effects become an integral part of the story telling in films, producers need to be more clued up about how to use visual effects to achieve the things required to tell the story, being smart about the use of visual effects combined with in camera effects can not only create a realistic look and feel to the shot but also done on budget too.
 It also helps to have that knowledge to be able to confidently negotiate when sending tenders out to VFX facilities to quote on your film."
- Hasraf 'HaZ' Dulull, Visual Effects Supervisor, Visual Effects Producer,
   www.about.me/hazvfx

"With the ever increasing use of digital effects in the production process, every producer should be armed with as much information as possible. Knowledge of how each department in a VFX pipeline needs to work together will be a saving in time and money. How can you afford not to read this book?"
- Will Rockall, RockKiss Digital Media Entertainment,
   http://www.rockkiss.co.uk

Introduction

Why this book is important

I wrote this book for you, I know that may sound like a trite way to start a book, but having worked in VFX for over ten years I realised that there was a definite need for this book. Whatever medium you are working in, whatever stage in your career you are in, you as a producer hold such a pivotal role and the success or failure of the project will come down to the decisions you choose to take and those you choose not to take.

In practice there are two reader groups for this book, both of which can be described as producers. On the one hand there are 'producers' who are responsible for the entire movie, film, game, TV show. Their remit is broad and could cover everything from casting to distribution. The other reader group this book is aimed at is the 'visual effects producer' or the 'CG producer'. Their focus is more precisely aligned with specific visual effects (hereon in referred to as VFX) or CG (same as CGI – computer Generated Image) issues. The book will give broad coverage to both groups of producers but will then split into specifics for each of them as their considerations vary greatly.

You may have the best computers and IT infrastructure, you may have a team of talented and dedicated artists, you may even be lucky enough to have a substantial budget to play with. There is of course a fourth ingredient to guarantee success - success defined as delivering the VFX or CG to standard on time and to budget - and that is your knowledge and in depth understanding of how the VFX/CG pipeline works.

This book is written for you the producer, whether you a starting on your journey or whether you are already an accomplished producer. Understanding exactly what considerations are involved for your whole team will help you deliver the VFX successfully. Whether it is across film, games, TV, visualisation, websites or mobile platforms, you as a producer will not be able to take your VFX team to every meeting or consult them on every email where you have to agree something with your client. It is your understanding of what they do that will have huge ramifications on how the shots will progress (or otherwise) down the pipeline.

This book is written for you the producer who has the most amazing technical team around you whose advice is overwhelming, intimidating and contradictory. This book is so you can understand what your team are saying to you and make a decision on what is best for the project and not based on who is shouting the loudest.

This book goes beyond theory and background of VFX, there are already many excellent books that can provide a background of the origins of VFX. From my own research this is the only book that will

- look at every aspect of VFX and CG from a producer's point of view,
- telling you what you the producer need to know about that task,
- how you can plan for it,
- what considerations you need to be aware of
- and what ramifications your decisions will have on the process.

Throughout the book I will be using examples borne from real life experiences (names, dates, numbers all changed to protect the innocent), there will also be guest contributions from expert specialists in certain areas

To start the book I would like to show you excerpts from job descriptions from many of the top VFX companies.

Skills
Have a good understanding of what can be achieved using top end software packages such as Maya, Renderman, Houdini, Nuke and Silhouette so as to work effectively with a highly technical and creative team of artists.

Have excellent and proven digital film and broadcast project management skills within a VFX facility.

Have a strong technical understanding of the visual effects industry and what is required both within CG and Compositing to enable the clients requirements to be met on time and within budget.

Again another job advert for a VFX producer from a major FX house

- Ability to manage and cater for client expectations
- Thorough understanding of CG production pipelines and post production in general

And one more to press the point

Provide schedules to artists and ensure they understand and are able to achieve their targets.

Understanding VFX/CG is more and more becoming a prerequisite for producers across any budget range across any platforms. Today for VFX and CG producers it's absolutely essential to even get an interview.

Having worked in VFX and games for almost fifteen years I have had the privilege to work with some very good producers. Producers who understand the VFX process and understand how artists, programmers and TDs (Technical Directors) work and thrive. Sadly there are producers who are clueless about film and game, let alone all the intricacies and gathering together all the disparate elements to successfully deliver a shot. Successfully delivered shots equal successfully delivered sequences. Unsuccessfully delivered shots mean sequences not being delivered, late nights and weekends being worked by all - except by the uninformed producer of course.

VFX and CG Survival Guide for Filmmakers and Producers

The days of a dedicated crack unit of CGI/VFX artists bailing out the uninformed producer are now gone. Producers are expected to know what they are doing otherwise the CG team will lose confidence in them immediately and start to steer the ship themselves.

The aim of this book is

- to teach you whether you are fledging VFX producer or an established film producer about the VFX process so that you will understand what VFX people are telling you
- to decipher all the technical jargon that you have comprehend to make a decision
- the questions you will need to ask and answer
- to understand the workflows and dependencies that you will have to keep open and flowing
- to schedule a show using these dependencies
- to pitch and win contracts for work
- to help to work with a range of clients with varying knowledge of the process
- to successfully implement CGI/VFX into your project and how to engage a VFX facility
- to budget successfully all the CGI/VFX requirements for your project

This isn't a theory book on VFX, there are many excellent theoretical books which deal with the history and craft of VFX, they certainly have their place. This book is a practical guide to the issues that you will have to face on a day to day basis. I will take you through worked examples, showing how your decisions can take projects down a myriad of paths.

Why is there such a problem with producers in the VFX industry?

Unlike many other industries VFX, CG, animation, post production (whichever field you're working in or looking to work in, I'm going to use the terms interchangeably in many instances I'm using them to mean the same thing from hereon in) has no accreditation facility. Anyone can claim to be a producer.

16

Imagine if other business sectors behaved in this way. Imagine your dentists fumbling around with the various instruments not knowing which way round to hold a periodontal probe. Imagine an accountant learning about the tax penal system on your accounts, a lawyer arriving in court expecting to figure out contract law as he goes along. Those industries wouldn't tolerate it. But in the VFX industry there is no accreditation system. And yes, while this also applies to artists, artists have to come armed with showreels, shot lists and it is very quickly apparent whether they know what they're talking about in an interview.

I am going to break this book down into several sections. *Part one* will go through what I call producer essentials, telling you what you need to know about what each department does, how it affects you and how you affect them. This can be thought of as a *'where do I start?'* section for those producers who can easily feel overwhelmed by the whole process about to unfold ahead of them.

Part two will look at the scheduling and the pipeline process and how each department will feed another. How dependencies are created and how you as a producer can keep the flow of digital assets open between them and minimise any downtime. We will look at some solid case studies and see how the considerations change from animation to film/TV to games.

Part three will focus on producer practicalities, what to do when you walk into a new studio or inherit a project, what to do when disparate software solutions have to be integrated together and go through a case study where your decisions and their consequences will be plotted out. What your options are when you choose to specialise in particular disciplines and present strategies for you to respond to the changing requirements of the project.

Part four will look at low/no budget film making, can you still afford VFX in your movie/TVC/game? Of course you can, I will show you considerations and planning you can take to minimise any extra costs in the post production stage, from script stage to talking with your actors and DOP to keep the shots passing through the post phase with minimum fuss.

Part five will close the book with a set of golden rules for producers derived from lessons learned from the rest of the book.

All the examples from the book have come from over ten years of experience and working with many different producers across a range of platforms from film to game, from short TV commercials shot in stereo to huge live events (including the London 2012 Olympics – in terms of live events, it doesn't get any bigger than that).

So without any further ado let us begin our journey…

VFX and CG Survival Guide for Filmmakers and Producers

Part 1 - Producer Essentials

Concept art & story boarding essentials

Concept art and storyboarding will give you different information and will require artists with different skillsets.

The concept art will
- layout the look and feel of the shots
- define a colour palette
- it will tell you about how the shot will be lit
- tell you who the characters are and what do they look like,
- tell you about the environment/environments, their scale and how much work will be involved to model all of these
- highlight the effects requirements

Fig 1.1 image from Corporal Punishment – writer/director Farhan Qureshi, artist Kelvin Johnson, © Farhan Qureshi 2012

VFX and CG Survival Guide for Filmmakers and Producers

*Fig 1.2 Images courtesy of Vincent Jenkins, ©
http://vincentjenkins.blogspot.co.uk/*

After you have appreciated the beauty in the concept art, you as a producer will have to list, budget and schedule all the elements required, do not worry if you do not understand the terms I am about to list, they will all be covered in this chapter. From Fig 1.1 you can see that you are going to need to have

- a crowd simulation,
- a lot of environment,
- rain effects,
- cloth effects if the umbrellas get blown around.

From the second and third images you should an effects requirements for

- the fire embers and
- the rain pelting downward.

The second image will also need work from the DMP (digital matte painting) department. The final image shows a lot of animation required, yes animation does not necessarily mean cute characters, cars need to be animated. The two main elements here are the cars and the environment. This is a wide environment so take into consideration the time it will take to render also there is a substantial DMP requirement. Notice in all of these shots the rigging requirement is quite low, this will change as soon as we introduce characters.

The storyboard deals with sequences of shots, it will tell you

- how many shots you will need in the sequence
- what elements you need and how often these elements will be used, this in turn will help you schedule your CGI artist's time accordingly, e.g. if a character is in every shot and a certain prop is only in one shot, you will want to allot more of the CGI artist's time to model and develop that character who appears more frequently than the prop which is seldom seen
- range of motion in the shot, this can be camera motion, character animation
- FX requirements, as well as character and environment you will know when specific effects like water, rain, fire, smoke etc. will be needed.

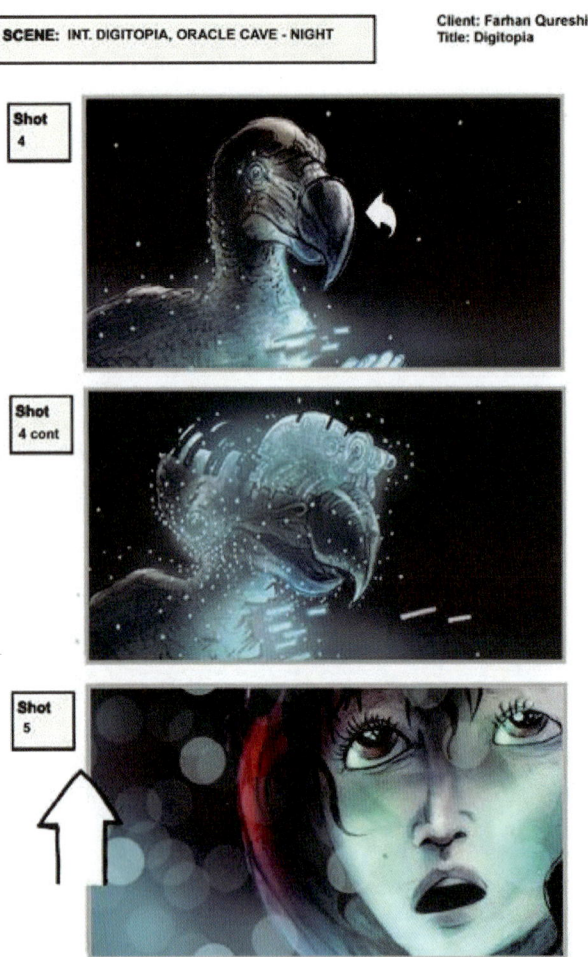

Fig 1.3 Concept Art from Digitopia: Discover Me – director: Farhan Qureshi, Artist: Stephen Trumble, © Farhan Qureshi 2010

There is more to concept art and storyboarding than the creation of beautiful images the information that you will see here will be the basis of planning out all the subsequent CG/VFX tasks. It will be useful when communicating exactly what you are looking for. Using the concept art together with an art style guide will create enormous efficiencies further downstream in the production process.

Previz essentials

A natural extension from storyboarding is previz (short for previsualisation), the process of blocking your shots and putting them together on a time line to see how well they play. Essentially you can quickly pose the characters in a series of key poses and create a composition using a virtual camera. You can quickly and cheaply render out these shots (a process you will commonly hear as 'playblasting' or 'flipbooking'). Stringing these individual shots together you can then create a sequence of shots and start to assess how well the shots work together.

The process allows animators and editors to work together and make a sequence in the fraction of the time and cost of a final version. Note that you can also previz the camera by using a handheld camera and walking it around the previz to create dynamic camera movements at an early stage.

There are cheaper alternatives to previz, called animatics, a process of putting your storyboards into a timeline in an editing programme. You can then play a sequence of storyboards as a movie and assess how the sequence is going to work, rather than looking at them on a board.

Whether you chose to previz or create an animatic you will be in a much better position to quantify your shots, know their duration and what elements will be involved further down the line. Doing a previz will indicate any additional elements that may have been missed out in the script breakdown. For instance you may find out that a series of shots of a plane taking off will require animation for the plane, modelling of a large terrain, lots of smoke and dust kicked off the ground.

It is easy to fall into the trap of thinking that previz is a luxury and not a necessity, especially when faced with a limited budget. Take time to work out the actual cost of previz, yes it will take off a reasonable proportion off your budget before any shots are started - but it will also help you refine and distill your shots to increase the quality of the final piece and reduce the cost further down the line through the various departments that will be put together (as we will see).

Match moving essentials

Matchmoving may be an entry level role but without doing this properly your whole sequence will fall apart. Matchmoving is essentially creating a virtual camera to match the real world camera which filmed any given shot.

Imagine you were placing a static CG space trooper into a moving shot. If your virtual camera which you will use to render out the space trooper didn't match the real camera you would find

- the trooper's perspective did not match the perspective of the shot and
- that the CG element would slide across the screen and would not stay in the same relative position that you are expecting.

Now imagine the character is moving and you can quickly see how none of the character's movement would match the geometry he is supposedly interacting with.

Fig 1.3 in both images the trooper is in the same 3D position only the camera has been moved to line/match him up correctly. Left - with the camera lined up incorrectly, right - with the camera correctly aligned so the character fits on the steps properly. Image © Farhan Qureshi, 2012

Depending upon the number and complexity of the shots you will either be hiring a matchmover or a matchmove department.

The matchmover(s) will matchmove a given shot in two distinct phases.

Phase 1 – they will track the plate, this is a pure 2D task where the matchmover will take the footage and find distinct features in the environment to track. The features will themselves remain stationary, but as the camera moves the feature will move across the screen (even though it is itself stationary). When the matchmover has tracked enough static features the matchmoving software will create a camera solution, known as a *solve*. This solve is essentially creating a virtual camera that exactly matches the movement of the real world camera used to film the backplate.

Fig 1.4 Even if you are not able to put tracking markers onto your footage you can still find sharp distinct features for the matchmovers to track. Here the lettering, the sharp edges on the staircase and the

25

overhead walkway will help create a stable camera solve.

Phase 2 – is to prove that this 'solved' camera is accurate. The camera will be imported back into your 3D application and be placed into a set that you know to be accurate. Either the client will provide detailed measurements of the set or you will go and record these. These measurements will either be drawn out or obtained by a digital scan of the environment to create 3D geometry. Either way you will bring in your solved camera from phase 1 into your 3D software and place it in accordance with the geometry.

Approving matchmoves

The output from the matchmove department will be a virtual camera which will be passed off to all the downstream departments (animation, lighting, effects etc). The camera that is output will be released into the shot for others to use therefore you will need a sign off process for approving matchmoved cameras.

There are various methods to check the matchmoved virtual camera is correct. Use a system whereby you render out static geometry placed into the 3D scene. Usually cones placed so that their tips are lined up with distinct features of the geometry, are a very good way to assess that the virtual camera will give an accurate rendering of any other 3D elements to be placed in scene.

When scheduling your shots you will find that without an approved matchmoved camera many of the downstream departments will not be able to begin the shots properly. Make sure that this part of the process is signed off and that the cameras are exported for other departments to gather in. If you do not you may lose valuable artist and render time further down the line.

Another consideration for scheduling purposes is to look at the complexity of the camera move and the suitability of the backplate. Firstly very fast moving cameras will exhibit extreme levels of motion blur making it very difficult for matchmovers to lock onto any distinct features to track. This will compromise the accuracy of the solve they will expect and will be difficult to gauge how accurately any virtual objects (cones) adhere to the geometry. By the same token if the move is so extreme that you cannot be sure the cones are sticking to the geometry then the reverse also holds that you cannot be sure that any virtual objects are not adhering to the real world geometry.

Secondly the backplate may not have any distinct features that the matchmover can use to create a track. If this is the case the matchmover will be manually moving a lot of tracking points him/herself to get any kind of solution out of the software. The matchmovers will be estimating pixel size movements to create a solve - the final result will be subject to as much accuracy estimation on the part of the supervisor as the matchmover who has provided the solve.

Remember that the matchmover has spent a lot of time on a difficult shot and quite naturally will want to have the shot signed off and taken off their schedule. The supervisor will take the opposite view and want the camera pixel perfect. It is your job to balance the two counter viewpoints. Essentially yes you do want a one hundred percent accurate solve but remember that the reason this solve is proving problematic is that there is a lack of raw data for the matchmover to create a solid solution.

Fig 1.5 here there is virtually nothing for the matchmover to track in the foreground and mid-ground, shots that contain barren landscapes like snow or sand are notoriously difficult to track and to approve, you should weigh up whatever extra time is spent on these shots versus the total number of shots in the schedule.

How much time can you realistically expect to allocate to a shot that will never really be one hundred percent accurate? How many shots are left to do? Take a view of the real cost of improving the accuracy of an impossible shot by a percent or two versus having multiple unsolved shots.

Modelling essentials

Even modellers can struggle to keep pace with all the advancements in techniques and software. You as a producer need not be an expert in parametric modelling but having a core understanding of the issues faced by your modelling team will help you plan efficiently and help avoid downstream dependencies that will come back to haunt you later in the show.

Modelling can be categorised between hard surface vs organic. You will find modellers who intrinsically prefer one to the other, think modelling space ships vs modelling humans.

Fig 1.6 In this image we can see both organic (the lady, the dress the hair) and hard surface (the case, the buckles, the shoe) modelling techniques. Image (c) Ben Godi 2012 www.selwy.com www.ben-godi.com

Modelling does not just end in modelling a surface a modeller may also be expected to know how to layout UVs, texture and in some instances have intermediate rigging and animation skills which we will discuss below.

Can the project progress if the model is unfinished?

There isn't a 'yes' or 'no' answer here, certainly there are some dependencies in the pipeline that require a fully finished model before they can begin. Others parts of the pipeline can either partially or fully continue without a fully finished model. You need to understand how your pipeline will function and when a final model can be substituted in place of a proxy model.

A character rig (see the next section) can be started and functionality built on an unfinished model. The finished model can be substituted in when it is approved, at which stage the character rig and skinning (the process of attaching the rig to the model) can be finalised. However you do not necessarily have to wait for a final model to be signed off before these downstream departments can begin.

Certainly how far you want to take this approach is a matter that you will need to discuss with the VFX/CG supervisor and subsequently schedule the amount of preparation work that can be done downstream.

Once a final model has been approved the various downstream departments, in particular rigging, texturing and even shading (see the following sections) can be progressed from development to final.

Rigging Essentials

When the model has progressed sufficiently enough it can be integrated into what is called a character rig. A character rig essentially is a skeleton of bones and joints. This skeleton is attached to the model and allows the model to be manipulated/brought to life by an animator. The rig is actually a set of controls that are linked to the bones and joints which further speeds up and aids the animation team. The rig can still (although it is not wholly recommended) undergo further iteration during the animation phase to add further functionality required by the animator. Make sure that any further changes of the rig will not invalidate any work done by an animator as this will result in time lost by the animator and further you will have to schedule in time for the animator to redo the shots with the new rig. If this happens more than once there will be some serious questions to answer as to why you let this happen, i.e. why did the schedule allow animation to begin when the rig was still being significantly changed?

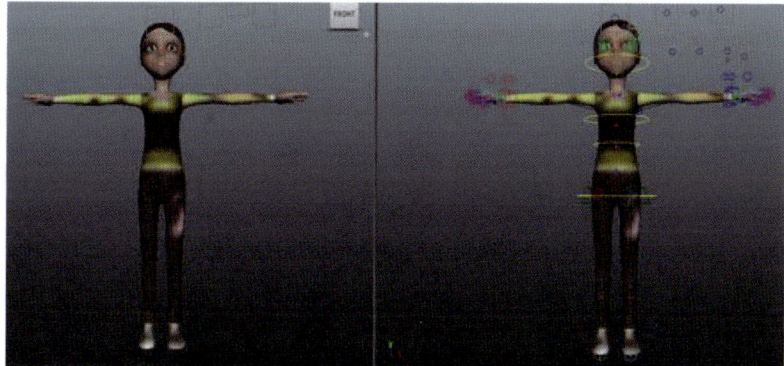

Fig 1.7 The two models are identical, the model on the right has a set of controls known as a rig. By manipulating these controls the character can be posed, when these poses are transitioned over time animation is created. Image (Fig. 1.7, 1.8, 1.10): Image © Farhan Qureshi 2012, model: J Doubles

While sign off and approvals are your friends, you need to keep the channels open and the schedule flexible enough to allow for change requests to the rig. The change request needs to be tightly managed, the changes will most likely come from the animation department as feedback notes are given to them for more complex animation which the original rig was not designed for.

If you are quite advanced in your schedule that incorporating such a change would cause the rig to become destructive, i.e. the old animations do not produce the same results on the new rig, then consider branching off to a multiple rig system. Branching is the process whereby, in this example, you have separate rigs with distinct sets of requirements. This can potentially cause problems for animators as they may be inconsistencies in which rig they are using for each shot/sequence. You should now be able to see why the use of previz is so important to establish the rigging requirements at the start before any shots are begun.

What you need to know as a producer is that the model will be the basis of any asset that will pass through the VFX pipeline. When that model is complete other artists can then feed into it to make it usable for an animator and lighter.

Texturing essentials

Texture artists will paint textures like skin colour, blemishes, eye colour etc. onto human models, on hard surface models for instance, on bridges they will paint on concrete textures, rust, graffiti etc. If you want any kind of pattern painted onto anything then these are the people you will need.

The texture artist is going to need a set of UVs laid out on the model. UVs are a coordinate system much like an XY coordinate system that you learnt to draw graphs on at school. However X, Y and Z are reserved for the 3D workspace, e.g. the character moves ten units in the X direction or the tank is nine units tall in the Y direction. Z is usually reserved for depth, i.e. the axis that goes in and out of your screen.

U and V are coordinate systems that are reserved for texture space. To use a quaint example think of dress making, the dress doesn't come fully assembled. When you make a dress you lay out all the separate parts out, the sleeves, the back, the neck line, hem etc. and then stitch them together.

When texturing an asset it is important to lay that 3D asset out in a flat plane so you can then apportion various textures to that character.

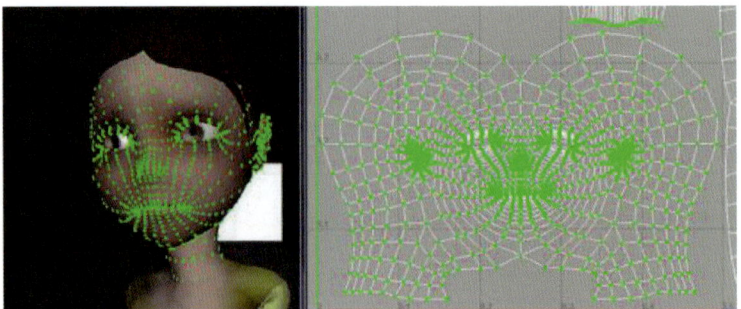

Fig 1.8 here the Libra model 3D head is unwrapped on the right to show its shape. The unwrapped shape is called its UV layout on which you would apply a UV map. By unwrapping the head you can place a texture on it.

Note here it is more than just colour information that you can lay out in this UV workspace, details such as bump and displacement maps (how much an area protrudes from the surface), normal maps (a fast way to calculate and manipulate the lighting) can also be assigned on the UV map.

The texture artist will need the UV map as an input to their process. Their job is to paint textures onto the map. It is important for you as a producer to assign this work to someone, either the texture artist or more likely the modeller.

An important point to note here is that UV layout is slowly being phased out as new software is being developed to streamline this lengthy and sometimes awkward process. These new methods will allow modellers or texture artists to paint directly onto the model without the need of painting in a 2D work space. While these softwares are slowly being implemented it will be some time yet before it is widely adopted across the whole industry and at many lower budgets.

Shading Essentials

Also known as surfacers, these people write complex code that describe how a surface reacts to light, is it shiny, does it reflect light (if so, how?), does it absorb light, does it emit light..? The code or network of nodes they output will be known as shading networks. Animation can still continue but these shaders are needed for lighting and rendering to begin.

Shading will go hand in hand with the Look Development process which we will discuss shortly. As its input the shading will require a reasonably close to finished model, including a UV layout and some degree of texturing. The shading can then be developed along side the look development and both will then feed into the rendering phase.

VFX and CG Survival Guide for Filmmakers and Producers

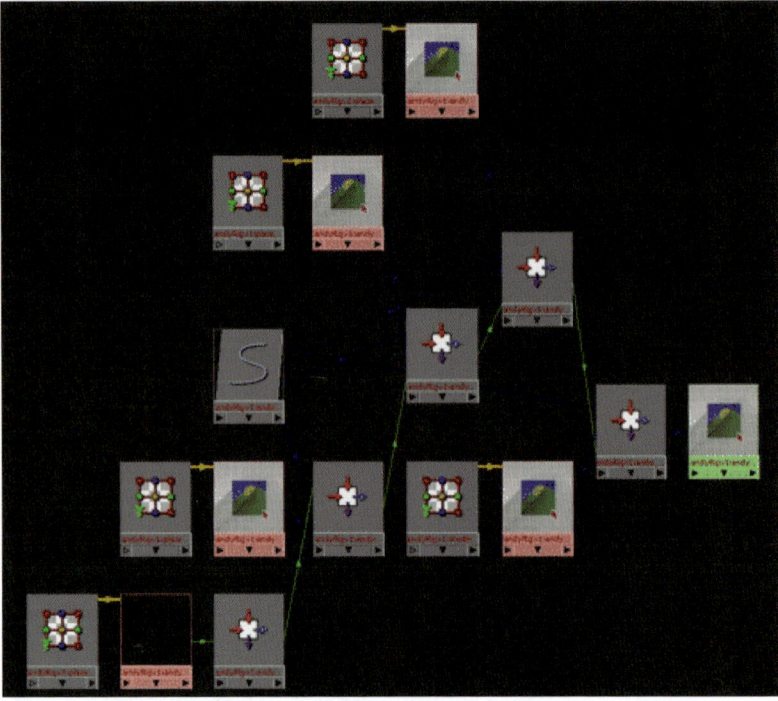

Fig 1.9 a simple shading network can comprise many interconnecting nodes, each node acts as a modifier to the one it takes an input from (in this case left to right). This nodal approach is extremely powerful as the shader writer can isolate parts of the graph to make changes which propagate through the structure. Many softwares are now built entirely on this nodal philosophy.

Animation and motion capture essentials

From people outside the industry animation has become a catch-all term for the whole VFX pipeline. It is probably the most visible part of the pipeline where anything from winged horses to talking bears immediately impose the feeling of computer involvement and abstraction to the viewer. But animation can also be subtle and in places that does not bring any attention to itself. Anything that needs to move in some simple way is also considered as animation, be it passing traffic to adding an extra character into the background. You as a producer should consider that props, vehicles and machinery will be part of your animation budget too.

Whilst we have mentioned how pipelines between modelling, rigging, texturing and shading can all exists somewhat in a state of flux, you will be wise to ensure that the model and the rig are completed or as near to completion as you can get them before animation is started. Texturing, shading and look development can run in parallel to the animation. The main outputs from animation will be lighting and subsequently rendering. Effects are also dependent to some degree on animation, any effects that occur as a direct result of animation, e.g. horses running kicking up dirt or any chains on an animated character will need to have the final animation passed onto the effects team.

Motion capture vs Animation

Motion capture is the process whereby real actors play the parts of animated characters on an adapted film set. The motion of the actors (be they humans or animals or anything else that can move) is recorded and then relayed back into the animation system. This set of data can be a direct replacement for the traditional form of animation or can be used in conjunction with existing animation.

In the early days of motion capture the data that was output was so noisy i.e. there were lots of distortions en-route from the recording session to importing the motion capture data into a 3D package, that the amount of clean-up required to make the data usable was more than if an animator had hand animated the sequence from scratch. Nowadays the turnaround of inputting the motion capture data into a 3D animation package is a lot quicker and allows for so much more flexibility, animators may even blend takes from different shoots or even blend with their own animation.

You as a producer will need to cost the amount of time it would take an animator to animate a sequence versus the cost of arranging a motion capture shoot. A big consideration is just how many shots are to be animated, if there are dozens of shots then you can see how using a mocap studio would save you time and money. However if there are a relative few shots to be animated, the cost of hiring out a motion

VFX and CG Survival Guide for Filmmakers and Producers

capture shoot will far outweigh the cost of having a couple of animators for a few weeks. While you can record a lot more animation on a motion capture shoot than a team of animators could animated, bear in mind that the data they send you back will still need to be integrated back into your timeline. Check with the motion capture facility what exactly they will give back to you and what they need from you in terms of rigged models.

Digital Matte Painting and HDRI

Digital Matte Painting is also known as DMP, this is the process of painting a stationary backdrop which will have all the other elements composited onto. Think of this as the background, it could be a horizon, a sunset, a cityscape. For exterior shots a lot of the time it will have a skyline which will help define the time of day. This will then be used in conjunction with the lighting and look development. There may be some back and forth working between the teams to arrive at the final aesthetic, for instance if the DMP was changed from a sunset to a night time full moon then all the lighting will have to be redone to match. The role of a DMP artist is a specialist one, normally done by someone from a fine art background who has made the move across to digital.

Fig 1.10 here the background skyline would be made up of a digital matte painting that would be composited behind the foreground and midground elements.
© *http://vincentjenkins.blogspot.co.uk/*

There are also stock libraries both freeware and subscription based where you can obtain pre-fabricated skyscapes and readily drop into your composites. Note also that the skyline used can directly be used as an input to a special light, called an *environment light*. The image can be translated into what is known as a High Dynamic Range Image (HDRI) which allows the lighter to accurately capture the direction of the incoming light.

VFX and CG Survival Guide for Filmmakers and Producers

Fig 1.11 Here the images of the sky have been stitched together to form an image which can be fed into an environment light to provide real world lighting conditions. © Owen Boyer, www.HDRMill.com

Note also that in stylised projects these HDRIs could be painted as well as photographed, in these cases the most likely candidate to paint a HDRI would be a DMP artist.

Effects essentials

Think of effects as essentially any moving thing that is not a character, a prop or environment. Effects can be thought of as natural phenomena such as smoke, fire, water or man-made like explosions, battlefield effects. A lot of shows will be effects centric, i.e. they may not need any modelling or animation and will be based on adding effects into live action, where it is impractical to have smoke, fire, explosions etc. on set.

In simple terms effects may be broken into three distinct categories which have quite separate considerations

Particle effects

These are anything that can be considered as particles either behaving independently or as a cohesive whole for example characters running through sand or snow. The resultant sand or snow that is kicked up are individual grains that start as one single clump but very quickly break up into their constituent individual particles. Other examples of fine particulate matter can be dirt, bullet impacts, snow, dust, smoke, rain etc. as well as more complex manufactured effects such as explosions, force fields, water wakes etc.

Instancing is a method whereby geometry can be substituted onto particles. This allows for a simplified rigid body simulation (see below for more on rigid body simulation) and can be used for debris and destruction effects where collision accuracy need not be as accurate as a full rigid body simulation. Instancing allows simulation time to be much faster.

Fig 1.12 using sprites (flat planes with textures that always face the camera) on particles is a versatile method for creating the illusion of snow or dust with very fast render times. In games sprites has been the preferred method

Fluid simulation

    This as you may imagine allows the simulations of fluids, but also in many softwares includes gaseous effects (in one widely used software, the fluid solver is primarily used as a gaseous solver). Pretty much all simulation packages will allow particles and fluids to interact to varying degrees, but the most advanced simulation tools will use particles as a basis for controlling the fluids thorough a process called meshing. This approach allows the artist the speed and full controls they are used to working with particles and adds an extra layer of control on top by allowing the fluids to take their underlying shape and behaviour from the particles.

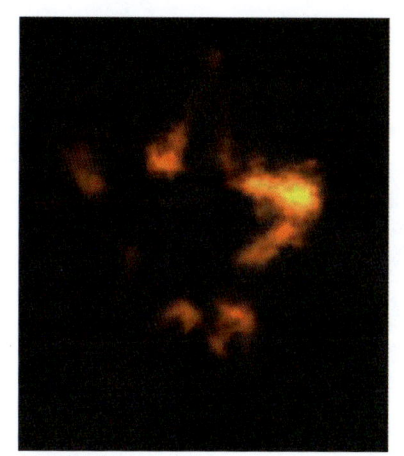

Fig 1.13 one of the most common uses of fluids in many software packages is to create smoke and fire - these types of phenomena cannot be animated in the same way as characters and props. Image: Farhan Qureshi © 2012

Rigid body simulations

This is the simulation of physics on geometry. As mentioned above you could use an instanced approach to particles, but a rigid body sim would be more appropriate when accuracy is important (think those big close up shots of structures collapsing) and the geometry involved is far more detailed and varied (an instanced particle effect would use geometry that is closer aligned in shape and size, think splinters or shards of wood where the pieces have roughly the same look and feel)

Cloth, feather, fur and hair

As mentioned earlier this could be considered as a character effect role but this largely depends on the individual shot/show. The reason this is considered an effects role rather than an animation role is due to the sheer number of elements involved (consider how many hairs are on a human head or feathers on a bird). The effects TD is responsible for setting up the behaviour of the cloth/feather/fur/hair so that it will respond to the individual demands of the character. These effects would be expected to interact with other effects such as a furry character interacting with water and going from a dry state to wet state.

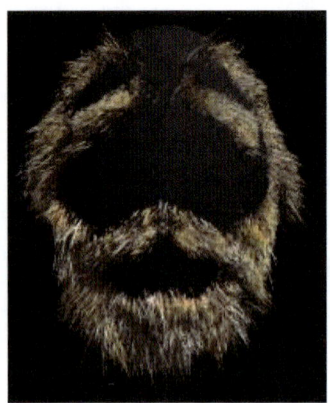

Fig 1.14 fur, image: Farhan Qureshi © 2012

Gathering Reference Materials

As with any of the disciplines getting reference images and videos is hugely important and will save a lot of time. To say to an effects artist I need an explosion without giving them any particular reference or description will mean your effects artist spending time making *a* perfectly fine explosion but not *the specific one* that you are looking for. Create a folder on the drive called reference and encourage everyone to fill it up with relevant effects, animation, lighting, models (videos, images, links) etc. From here you can point an artist to a particular piece of reference, you will be surprised at how much closer the artist will get with his/her first pass to what you are expecting to see.

What is the difference between effects artists and effects TDs?

A TD is short for Technical Director, a TD is responsible for building the shot gathering together all the disparate elements from animation to bringing in environments and props and the delivering the rendered final frames from all of these. An effects TD is a specialised TD who deals specifically with effects. An effects TD would set up effects rigs, similar to an animation rig that would be deployed across a team of animators, an effects rig would be deployed across a team of effects artists who would use it to create effects instead of animation.

Think of Spiderman shooting out webs from his wrists, an effects TD would create an asset with controls (known as parameters) that would allow an effects artist to manipulate depending upon the shots involved. Definitions vary from company to company but a useful rule of thumb is that a TD will create assets that an artist would use to complete shots.

Character effects

These are a special sub section of effects artists who deal with character specific effects including hair, fur and cloth, jewellery etc. that moves directly with the character. Although a lot of setup of these effects can be done before the model is completed a final setup would really be only production ready when a final model is ready to be attached to. Controls that the character effect artist would need to setup may need to be nested or linked to elements inside the character model and rig control hierarchy. In these cases the character effects artist and the rigger would need to work in close conjunction as each one's set up work will affect the other's.

Who lights, renders and composites Effects?

Effects is quite unique in many ways from the other disciplines we have discussed so far. One of its idiosyncrasies is that generally it may not be passed onto the lighting department to light and render as the animation, layout, crowd simulation etc. would otherwise be.

Depending upon the exact working of a studio it is not uncommon for an effect artist to light, render and composite their own work. There are some valid reasons for this, which are mostly practical. Unlike for example, animation, an effect to be signed off the VFX supervisor will need to see it rendered and usually composited against the backplate - this process is called slap comping, where the effect artist places the rendered sequence onto the backplates him/herself. The VFX supervisor is then able to give feedback and have the effect iterated without the need of a lighter and compositor.

When the effect has been finalled it will be passed onto the compositor as one of the elements they need to composite into the final shot. The VFX artist would have carried out a lot of the grading work for the compositor so make sure that their compositing script is available to the compositor to pick up.

Effects artists also have to consider texturing the effect themselves. It is worth breaking the effect into three distinct phases

1. Reference - gathering and agreeing on the reference materials
2. Previz - where the effect can be seen and assessed in its un-rendered simulation phase through the use of a playblast or filpbook
3. Visual target - where you take the agreed simulation and then apply textures and the lengthy process of rendering and the use of the render farm

By individually reviewing the work at these interim phases you have a better chance of the effect being signed off quicker and are able to flag any areas of concern earlier in the process.

Crowd simulation Essentials

Where does crowd simulation fit into your pipeline? Does it fit into your pipeline at all? As the name suggests this department is responsible for the simulation of crowd like behaviour, be it a marauding army, a school of fish or even a tornado of bats surrounding Bruce Wayne (a truly excellent example of crowd simulation). The crowd sim department is very dependent on having the correct inputs from various departments as we will see below. The crowd simulation department will deliver caches (see below) to the effects, cloth/hair and lighting department.

A cache is a set of data written out to disc, which when read from disc will produce the same result as the original simulation in a fraction of time - the fraction being determined by how quickly it can be read from the servers compared against how long it took to originally calculate the simulation. Regardless of your network speed the cache will give a stable playback of the effect without the need of any simulation. This is especially useful for when you are rendering the crowd simulation on the render farm. With any type of simulation the simulation will only execute correctly when played back sequentially. A render farm will not play back the simulation sequentially instead it will take individual frames and process them independently. Having the simulation embedded in a cache will ensure that the correct data and rendered without any corruption.

A crowd simulation uses rules to control a set of agents. An agent is a single entity that can choose how to traverse the environment in conjunction with many other agents. In the case that the agent is a human character, the crowd simulation TD will need

- a human model,
- a working rig and
- a set of predefined animations such as walk and running cycles, idle states, turning around, climbing animations etc. These can be either hand animated or from motion capture
- geometry for the ground plane and any obstacles/collision objects

There are broad based softwares that handle the whole process or there are very specific softwares that can handle one part of this process, for instance there are softwares that can provide falling and colliding animations when a stimulus is applied within a crowd simulation.

You will need to be aware of any geometry the agents are to manipulate. Typically you will need a ground plane for the agents' feet to traverse across and any obstacles that the agent needs to manoeuvre around or collide with. Your agents may not always be human or land based creatures, crowd simulation covers the behaviour that is exhibited from fish to birds such as bats (think of the truly excellent crowd sim on the bats in Batman Begins - they must have hired a truly talented crowd sim artist to do that work:), from cars to spaceships.

Worked example: a CG army lays siege to a CG city

Let us look at a complex example of the CG army invading a CG city and what as the producer you will have to make sure is available to your crowd simulation team. An army is at the outskirts of a fort trying to get in. You have as most battle sequences do, two opposing armies, in this example I'm going to substitute the army inside for a crowd of civilians without any weapons.

The army sling burning balls of fire over the walls with their trebuchets and penetrate the wall's defences. Inside the city the agents are responding to the stimulus of the fire balls that have landed inside the city. They run and flee in directions away from the fireballs. Outside the wall the army start climbing ladders to climb into the city. Here you as a producer will see the following inputs need to be provided to the crowd sim team

Downstream dependencies:
From modelling and layout
- geometry for the city, how tall are the outer walls?
- what is the layout for the interior city, where are the pathways, how wide or narrow are they?
- what obstacles do both the army and the civilians need to overcome?

Animation
- identify the main animations needed
- firing bows and arrows
- climbing up ladders
- queuing to climb up ladders...
- running aggressively towards target (soldier to civilian)
- running away from stimulus (civilian from soldier, civilian from fireball)

Effects
- identify static and dynamic objects,
- static objects won't be affected by the crowd sim but will affect the crowd sim, things like walls and hurdles which the crowd sim agents will have to negotiate
- dynamic objects are things that will be affected by the crowd sim, things like a collapsing fruit stall or a horse cart that could be trampled over and easily break.

Upstream dependencies:
Effects
- cloth and hair needs to be simulated, are there flags that the army are carrying, what cloth and hair do the various agents have?
- dust needs to be spawned (emitted) from agents
- is water involved? Rain splashes on agents, agents running though puddles
- where are the fireballs landing?
- blood
- if guns are being carried what weapon effects are needed, weapon fire (how many different types of muzzle flashes?), bullet impacts (how many different surfaces, concrete, brick, dirt, metal, human/blood?)?
- agents will be damaging the environment, modelling, animation and rigid body dynamics may need to be added.

You can see from this example that you as producer need to be identifying and scheduling work both upstream and downstream so that the crowd simulation team can begin to work on their shots.

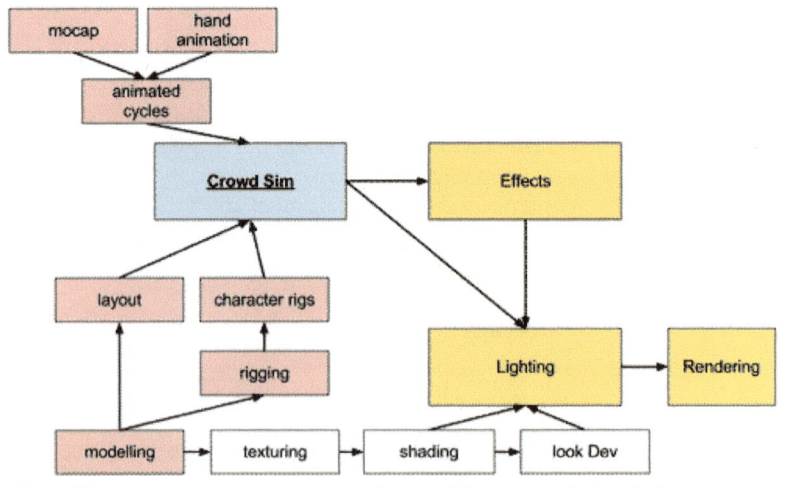

Fig 1.15 you as a producer can see how adding crowd simulation will increase the number of dependencies and will need to ensure the right packets of data are delivered to/from the right teams to ensure there are no blockages downstream.

Lighting and rendering essentials

A student asks a teacher why lighting is so important. The teacher shows the student a black frame - all your high res modelling, precise beautifully painted textured, long hours laboured over animation and wonderful effects simulation will all just be black frames if there are no lights added to the scene. Lighting is, as the name suggests is the placement of virtual lights to the scene. It is in this phase that you define the look and feel of the movie and can create a high polished epic or a cheap and cheerful low end cartoon.

Lighting has a big brother called Look Development. Look Development is the lighting that is done at the outset, before models, animation and effects are completed. The look development will create a look and feel that will be passed onto the lighting department to use in the actual production. In essence it can be thought of as creating a lighting template which can then be passed onto the lighting department to take over and implement in the final shot.

Lighting's other sibling is called rendering. If lighting is about artistic merit and expression, rendering is the technical tweaking of numbers to output the final frame at the highest quality in the fastest time possible. The lighter will be responsible for generating these numbers, but you as a producer have to think about how long it takes to render a shot to final quality.

What is the difference between a render that takes sixty seconds and one that takes ninety seconds?

Thirty seconds may be your answer, but the *real answer is 50% longer*.

When you translate that 50% extra per frame over the length of a sequence you are looking at turning a week's rendering into a week and a half. Extrapolate this further and you'll see how even by keeping a tight rein on every other department your rendering time could yet take you beyond the delivery date.

Working backwards from your delivery date will allow you to use these render times per frame to perform some basic calculations on when you would need to start the rendering to deliver a show finished on time. Unless you are doing a very short format show this calculation on its own will not suffice, for two reasons

i. your sequences should be broken into shots and these shots should be staggered in delivery, i.e. lighting on shot one should begin while animation on shot six is starting, you don't want to wait for all the animation to finish if the shots are independent of one another, start lighting as soon you can (the worked example on scheduling will go into a lot more detail on how to stagger all the processes and have them work together, for now I want you to understand the considerations involved) and

ii. is the topic of what are you going to render on? Read on for the answer to this specific question.

Lighting Passes

Ultimately the renders that come out of 3D will need to be adjusted in 2D otherwise known as 'in post/comp'. You may wonder why after all the effort that went into look development, lighting and optimising render times do you still need an additional work in 2D compositing.

There are many good reasons for this.

It is easier to make changes to the final look in 2D than it is in 3D. If you wanted to raise the levels or adjust the hue of a rendered image, you could go back into 3D and tweak multiple settings and then wait for the render to complete before knowing whether it was right or not. You can see what a lengthy process this becomes when you multiply that by several iterations. In 2D you can make changes quicker by using a slider. You are not in fact re-rendering any images you are applying adjustments to the rendered image. These adjustments are both more precise and quicker to calculate, they are also more intuitive to adjust.

To assist your compositing teams to make adjustments quicker you will need your lighters to render out images with several passes. By breaking an image up into several passes you are giving *granular* control to the compositors to precisely adjust for a given look. The compositor will save out these changes in what is called a 'script'. This script can then be shared around the whole department, created as a default to ensure a sequence of shots all have the agreed look.

VFX and CG Survival Guide for Filmmakers and Producers

Fig 1.16 this is known as a beauty pass, this beauty pass can be separated out into a number render passes. Image courtesy of RockKiss © http://www.rockkiss.co.uk/ from the film Metamorphosis 2012

When separated out the beauty pass can be recreated by putting together all the various passes. Your compositor can now apply adjustments to any of these layers to create make precise adjustments to the image faster than it would take a 3D lighter to re-render.

51

VFX and CG Survival Guide for Filmmakers and Producers

Fig 1.17 from top left to bottom right, the passes are alpha, depth, diffuse, normal, ID, illumination, specular, vector and world points.

Render Farms

Rendering is a source of great contention. It is in theory an automated process but nothing is further from the truth. Rendering and the process of managing rendering is a very human task and involves a massive amount of human intervention to get the machines to behave the way you want them to and to avoid the other artists from abusing the farm and getting their own shots through at the expense of others. You as a producer will have to be very clear on what is to go on the farm, who has priority and how you divide the farm up between teams and shows (who have their own producers).

So what is a render farm? Imagine if you would you have one hundred frames to render, each frame takes one minute to render. That is a hundred minutes to render the shot on one machine.

i.e. (100 frames * 1 minute)/1 machine = 100 minutes total render time

Imagine now you have two machines to render on, all of a sudden that one hundred minutes to render the shot takes fifty minutes.

52

i.e. (100 frames * 1 minute)/2 machines = 50 minutes total render time

Taking that analogy further, imagine having ten machines, now your rendering time is ten minutes for the whole sequence, not even enough time to get a cup of tea.

i.e. (100 frames * 1 minute)/10 machines = 10 minutes total render time

That was the whole idea behind render farms to give you this increase in render time.

Why is it important to be able to render faster?

Could you not just start it off at the end of the day and go home, come back in the morning and see how it looks? Well the answer is yes, but as with anything you can do faster, more is often expected. If you can render in ten minutes instead of a hundred, then you can do up to ten iterations of lighting, these iterations of lighting will increase the quality of the show - although there is a concept of diminishing returns when it comes to iterations. More iterations doesn't always mean better quality, just ask the weary artist who is on iteration 37, is it really that much better than iteration 36, 35 or even iteration 6? But the point holds, being able to do things faster allows you to spend more time iterating and achieving that sweet spot.

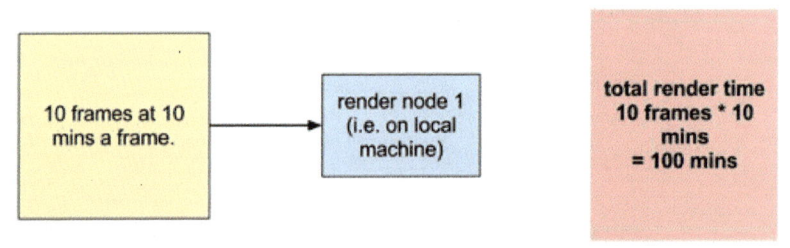

Fig 1.18 rendering on a local machine, 10 frames at 10 mins a frame = 100 mins total render time over one render node (i.e. on local machine)

54

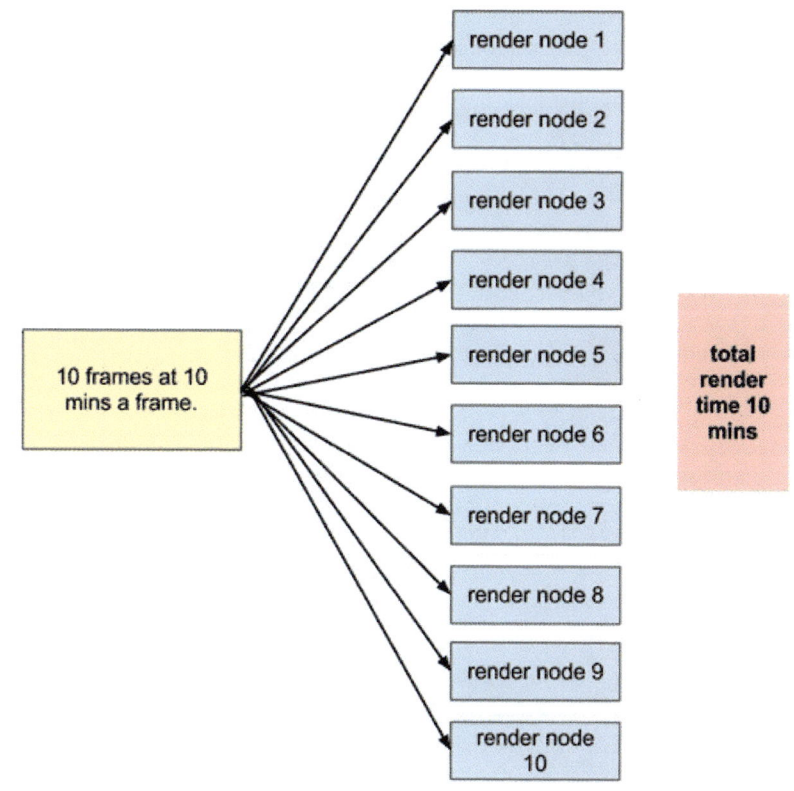

VFX and CG Survival Guide for Filmmakers and Producers

Fig 1.19 Same 10 frame sequence spread over 10 nodes means the same job could be done in 10 minutes

Multiple users on the farm

However when more people are involved the more complicated things quickly become - and with render farms that rate of added complication can grow exponentially.

Imagine now you have ten users with their hundred frame sequences all wanting it done in the next ten minutes. Well the answer is that your ten machine render farm is clearly not going to get everyone's renders back to them in ten minutes.

You as a producer are one of the key people involved in the brain's

VFX and CG Survival Guide for Filmmakers and Producers

trust who will decide how the resources are supposed to be split. Do you prioritise one person ahead of another and if so, how? Do you let everyone have an equal share of the farm (if so then why even have a farm - rendering on your own machine is as likely to return the sequence faster)?

This of course is an ideal situation, you will in practice have someone whose two frames take five hours to render each versus someone who has a thousand frames to render which take ten seconds (of course you may have a thousand frames taking five hours each). Everyone is going to be at different stages and have different requirements and everyone's work is important.

Some may be needed for immediate delivery for a client review, someone else's work may be needed as a team of other artists are sitting idly by dependent on these frames to render. These are all considerations that you have to take into account while at the same time have some IT boffin telling you about splitting the farm up into cores and assigned pools and workgroups.

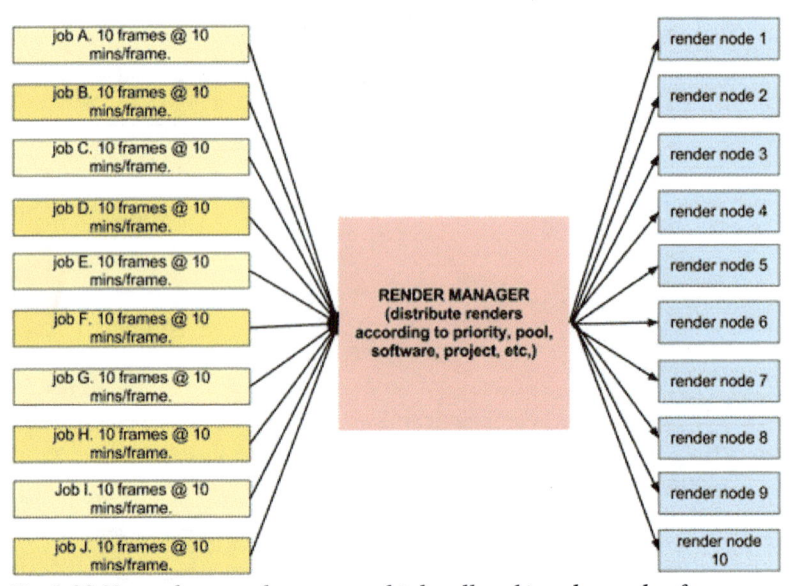

Fig 1.20 Now when you have several jobs all making demands of the render farm at the same time, jobs will be distributed to the farm based on a complex relationship based on priority, render pools, job allocations, software licences etc.

56

Now add to this the fact that you may very well be sharing this farm with other projects whose producers have different delivery demands and have a different understanding of priorities - essentially their priority is their own show and you could crash and burn for all they care. That is the reality of the situation. They are responsible for delivering their own show and you are responsible for yours. It is the person above you both who is responsible for delivering all the shows.

Farm Politics

A quick note on farm politics here, you as a producer may be working in a company where more than one project is being delivered simultaneously. The demands on a render farm are like London buses turning up, it can be all quiet for a long time and no buses will come along, then all at once ten will turn up at the same time. The same way the render farm will go through periods of under-use but then everyone will need to use it at the same time, everyone will have high priority and clients will be coming in on the same day.

There are many approaches to get your project through this period of over capacity from utilitarian to Machiavellian. Ultimately it is going to be someone's call to decide how the farm is divided up and priorities assigned. The number of variables here are enormous. Whilst collating the figures and presenting a business case will give you a position of authority it may not guarantee a favourable position on the farm. However the data you should be collating would include

- number of frames to render
- average render time per frame – can you group many frames together in one render and thereby save time by using only one node on the farm?
- software licences to be used
- number of downstream dependencies this render has (e.g. a crowd simulation needs to be cached on the farm, which will be passed onto the cloth and hair department, which will then go through lighting which will then go to comp)
- artist's hours already spent setting up the renders
- time until delivery
- overall budget of the shows – if one show has a budget ten times

the other, the potential loss of not delivering is more substantial

You can portion the farm into different render speeds, i.e. have different pools for fast renders and slow renders. By putting fast renders into one separate pool you can ensure that lighting TDs submit their renders in large batch sizes. This essentially means that you use a single blade (blade/node are used interchangeably, they refer to a *'single'* machine on which to render upon - note though that *'single'* machine can then be broken up into cores or processors, which is when things really get complicated - make sure you know how your render farm is and can be divided) on the farm to render out many quick frames, thereby

a. reducing the loading time on the blade – imagine you have a hundred frames to render that take ten seconds each. If you put these on a single blade, the blade loads the scene file once and then renders frames one to a hundred sequentially, i.e. taking 10 secs * 100 frames, i.e. 1000 secs, which is 16mins 40 secs. Under normal conditions you would spread this across ten or even a hundred blades and bring the render times down to potentially ten seconds for the whole sequence (plus whatever time it takes for the blade to load the scene file). But there are further considerations when there are multiple quick jobs, given below

b. If you have a fast rendering scene (say below ten seconds) then it would be faster for you to render all the frames (say a fifty) on a single machine. The reason is the load time, i.e. the time it will take the server to load the scene. It may be quite likely that opening the software and loading in the scene is longer than the time it takes to render. If this is the case then consider rendering all the frames on a single blade. This way you can be sure that the whole process time is spent on rendering not opening software and loading in scene files.

c. given it is a quick render not blocking the farm for other users, let's extend the analogy for a quick render to include anything below five minutes, now if every quick render was split across the multiple nodes on the farm, the farm would essentially be using all the blades to render single frames that took five minutes. What this would mean is that everyone now has to wait for a blade whether or not they had a quick render or a long render. By pooling the blades into fast and slow renders you can give top priority for fast renders on the fast queue and top priority for slow renders on the slow queue. When one of the queues is under utilised then the overflow from the other queue can go onto any unused capacity, e.g. if there are no slow renders queued all the fast renders can take over the whole farm until such time as slow renders are queued. When the slow renders come online they will take back the pool of blades designated for themselves and the fast renders will go back to queuing on the fast queue. They will of course go back to rendering onto the slow queue when the slow renders have finished.

d. when the farm is busy you will be stuck queuing (waiting for render blades to become available), by putting a hundred frames on one blade means that as soon as an artist gets that individual blade for themselves then no one can take it away from them and their renders are as good as done in whatever amount of time it usually takes. Contrast this to the spreading your renders out over a number of blades, it maybe that frames ten to twenty have to wait for a blade to become free while all the others are done. You could easily end up waiting for hours for a blade to become free to render out frames ten to twenty when the rest of the sequence was finished hours ago. By putting all your frames on one blade you only need to wait once and then once you have a blade it is just a simple calculation of

*time per frame * number of frames*

The essential principle here is that a farm can be split up into any set of criteria, not just based on the job. By isolating relevant criteria for your company you can ensure a fair usage policy for everyone concerned not just the show that is struggling. If a show is in such a state that it needs to have the entire farm to deliver on time then there are problems downstream, most likely originating from the producer that need to be addressed. Address these issues first rather than relying on the render farm to come to the rescue at other projects' expense, otherwise you will be falling back to this unsatisfactory solution again and again.

Compositing Essentials

In the case of live action you will need the renders that come out of the CG pipeline to be inserted on the filmed backplate. This process is called compositing and requires a specialist compositor whose skillsets are quite apart from the 3D CG and VFX skillsets that we have discussed in previous sections.

The compositing team sits right at the end of the pipeline and will be the most squeezed once deadlines start slipping or are missed altogether. In terms of forming a team you may be tempted to form the compositing department quite late as you wait for the renders from the CG team. While in practice this may sound sensible it is worth having a small compositing team working and testing all the elements from CG at an early stage. By doing this you can test and assess all the passes that have come out from lighting, see the animation and effects working on the backplate and make more accurate decisions based off these composited against a live backplate.

The same skillset of compositing can also be used in many of the early stages of a production, such as tidying up and preparing a plate to go into the CG pipeline. As renders gradually appear you can then ramp up the size of the compositing team to complete the sequences. By having a team in place before this will allow the pipeline from 3D to 2D to be finalised and some proven template scripts (a script here refers to a composite script which is essentially the same as a scene file for 3D CG teams) to be developed and distributed around the compositing department.

Consider also that the development work done early on by the compositing team will include decisions about colour grading and colour workspaces both of which will affect how the final look of the project will be and feed iteratively back into look development and lighting.

VFX and CG Survival Guide for Filmmakers and Producers

Part 2: Scheduling - getting shots through the pipeline and understanding dependencies

Case study 1: producing a short CGI film from scratch

I recently completed a short full CGI movie called Digitopia: Discover Me, the movie is six minutes long and I did all the 3D CGI. It took seventeen months to complete (this figure of seventeen months is made up of working in my spare time, i.e. after working crunch hours (more about 'crunch' and its ill effects and why it is completely unnecessary later), looking after a new born baby (yes it is possible, although not wholly advisable, to make movies after having babies) and all that entails - in truth if I could get half an hour work done a night that would be success).

Here is a list of tasks that need to be completed should you be crazy enough to undertake this endeavour on your own.

Stage 1: Preproduction
- write a script
- storyboard the script
- break the shots down into a list
- create an animatic
- concept art
- character design
- model and rig a character, environment and props
- previz
- texturing and shading

Stage 2: Production
- animation

- lighting
- rendering
- effects
- compositing

Stage 3: Post production
- editing
- sound design
- conform
- finishing and formatting

I have broken these down into three broad categories, depending upon your production some of these items may be moved to other phases. Generally if you adopt this approach you should cover the major milestones of your project and tie together all the dependencies in one part of the project allowing you to progress to the next stage of production.

In making a short animation film like this spending more time on the earlier pre-production items will

a. make the other two phases a lot more streamlined and
b. efficient and minimise any rework to do later

The temptation is to rush through preproduction and go straight into getting shots done. Rushing straight into production is like a dog chasing its tail, you will only end up going round in circles, having to relight and re-render animations that on the surface work well but do not work in the edit, also you will find that the rig only works for certain animation setups so you will have to develop it further, all the while you are trying to complete shots to a schedule.

You as a producer will need to take particular note of the animatic (which if you are wise will make it imperative to turn this into a Previz), this will tell you
* how many shots there are
* how many items need to be modelled
* What animation is needed
* What effects are needed
* How long a render of the sequence would take, i.e. sequence one is a hundred frames with several characters and environments,

sequence two is a thousand frames with one character etc.

With this information you can start scheduling, budgeting, allocating and identifying resources (software, computers and of course artists) that you will need.

Start identifying dependencies in your pipeline. If you can get a lower resolution model to get the rigging started you can then have animators start to previz while shading artists can start on look development on the shots. The higher resolution model can then be worked on and integrated back in time for production to begin.

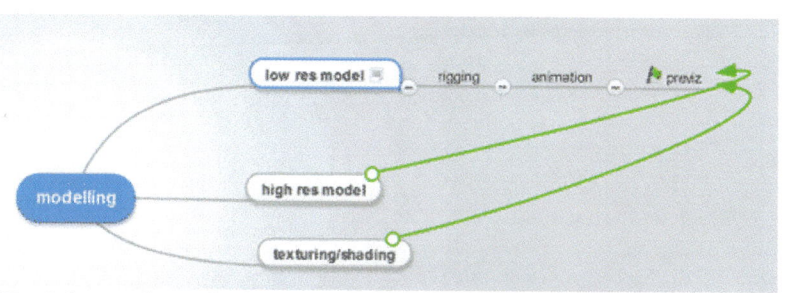

Fig 2.1 providing a higher resolution model with textures and shading won't affect rigging, animation or previz. This allows you to schedule the rigging, animation and previz in parallel to further modelling, texturing and shading.

Having a robust publishing system will allow the final previz to bring in the updated model, shaders and textures. A publishing system is a system whereby any changes to any part of the pipeline will be propagated through the pipeline. This is done in a semi-automatic manner and many publishing systems can be configured to meet the needs of your project, e.g. the system could send an e-mail to everyone working on a particular shot or in a certain department that an asset has changed. This could then trigger re-renders into someone's task list, also when opening up a scene file the publishing system can alert the user that certain assets (e.g. cameras, models, rigs, animations etc.) have been updated and allow the user to update to the latest asset iteration or roll back to a previous version.

You may be under pressure to skip the previz stage as some consider it a luxury. Under tight timelines it may be a luxury that your budget and schedule are unable to support. As a savvy producer you should make an effort to incorporate some previz into the schedule.   The great thing about previz is that you can go through it at a rapid pace as the animation quality does not have to be finalised and no lighting or rendering is required.   What previz will provide you is a near precise version of everything you will require thus minimising any unexpected tasks further down the line.

Start breaking the sequences into shots and label them.   In my short film I have seven distinct sequences.   I defined a sequence as '*a series of shots that either take place in the same location*' or '*a part of the story that has progressed the characters down the story line such that events are distinct from the previous shots and no continuity is required between the last shot of the previous sequence and the first shot of the next sequence*'.

	artist	day rate (£)	alloted days	total (£)	subtotal 1 (£)	subtotal 2 (£)
Concept Art						
designs of environement and props	concept artist	150	2	300		
character designs	concept artist	150	2	300		
colour schemes	concept artist	150	2	300		
initial look dev work	concept artist	150	2	300		
detailed storyboards	concept artist	150	2	300		
	Concept Art Total				1500	1500
	Department Total Concept Art				1500	1500
Modeling/Animation						
Character models						
Libra						
high res (zbrush)	character modeller	250	3	750		
med res (for Maya rig)	character modeller	250	2	500		
human						
high res (zbrush)	character modeller	250	2	500		
med res (for Maya rig)	character modeller	250	1	250		
mammoth						
high res (zbrush)	character modeller	250	3	750		
med res (for Maya rig)	character modeller	250	2	500		
dodo						
high res (zbrush)	character modeller	250	3	750		
med res (for Maya rig)	character modeller	250	2	500		
	Modelling Total				4500	4500
Animation Rigs						
Libra	Rigging TD	250	3	750		
Human	Rigging TD	250	2	500		
mammoth	Rigging TD	250	2	500		
dodo	Rigging TD	250	2	500		
	Rigging Total				2250	2250
Character Animation						
Blocking						
Libra	Animator	250	5	1250		
Human	Animator	250	1	250		
mammoth	Animator	250	3	750		
dodo	Animator	250	3	750		
Camera	Animator	250	3	750		
Final Animation						
Libra	Animator	250	5	1250		
Human	Animator	250	1	250		
mammoth	Animator	250	5	1250		
dodo	Animator	250	2	500		
Camera	Animator	250	5	1250		
	Animation Total				8250	8250
Environment						
environment cave	modeller	250	3	750		
props	modeller	250	1	250		
Console UI	UI Artist	250	3	750		
	Environment Total				1750	1750
	Department Total Modelling/Animation				16750	16750

Fig 2.2a isolate all the tasks that need to be done in terms of departments involved and the number of elements, insert the time spent and the cost per artist (figures arbitrary in this example)

FX

Particles

Transformation FX	FX TD (particles)	250	6	1500	
Ambient (Dust, breath, heat haze)	FX TD (particles)	250	2	500	
FX Total				2000	2000

Fur, Hair and Cloth

Libra	FX TD (Fur/Hair/Cloth Artist)	250	5	1250	
Human	FX TD (Fur/Hair/Cloth Artist)	250	0	0	
mammoth	FX TD (Fur/Hair/Cloth Artist)	250	5	1250	
dodo	FX TD (Fur/Hair/Cloth Artist)	250	2	500	
Fur, Hair and cloth Total				3000	3000
Department Total FX				**5000**	**5000**

Lighting

Shaders

Libra	Lighting TD	250	3	750	
Human	Lighting TD	250	1	250	
mammoth	Lighting TD	250	3	750	
dodo	Lighting TD	250	2	500	
Shaders Total				2250	2250

Lighting

Look Dev	Lighting TD	250	3	750	
Final Lighting + rendering	Lighting TD	250	8	2000	
Lighting Total				2750	2750
Department Total Lighting				**5000**	**5000**

Post Production

Visuals

Compositing	Compositor	200	3	600	
Editing	Editor	200	2	400	
Grading	Grader	200	2	400	
Film Out	Editor	150	1	150	
Visuals Total				1550	1550

Sound

Foley	Foley Artist	200	3	600	
Soundscape	soundscape Artist	150	1	150	
Score	Musician	100	2	200	
Sound Total				950	950
Department Post Production Total				**2500**	**2500**

Production

Producer	Producer	0	20	0	
Production coordinator	Production coordinator	0	20	0	
Director	Director	0	20	0	
Production Total				0	0
Department Production Total				**0**	**0**

mini movie Total		**30750**

Fig 2.2b this will give you a headline figure for the running cost of the project for one iteration. Note that further iterations will add expense (which is why it is so important to get reference and have regular reviews, see Worked Example – A Bear Walks Into A Bar in part 3 below) and does not include any fixed costs such as hardware, software, other business expenses like rent, lighting + electricity, heating etc.

To illustrate this I labelled sequence 1 as Libra outside the cave, sequence 2 as Libra entering the cave, sequence 3 Libra interacting with the machine and so on.

these phases are based on Libra's genreal locale and who she is interacting with			start frame	end frame
phase 0		**intro/prologue - anticipation of Libra entering**		
000_INTRO		desc		
	30	Libra moves forward	1	108
	40	bike approaches	1	48
	50	Libra scrambles	1	160
	80	CU on bike		72
	90	Libra backs up, sees the light	1	250
	100	CU on the light		48
	110	CU on Libra		81
	120	Bike leaves		72
	130	CU on Libra		
	140	Looking at the light		
	150	CU on Libra		168
phase 1		**Libra enters Cave, sees severs, moves forward**		
001_LEC_0010		Fade In Libra emerges from deep shadows		196
phase 2		**Libra gets to grips with the sever**		
002_LUS_0010		Libra considering approaching the arcade machine		168
002_LUS_0030		hand waggles joystick	1	192

Fig 2.3 Start breaking the sequences into individual shots that you can start to assign times to and to artists. It is possible to do this in a spreadsheet but there exists specialist scheduling softwares to do this more efficiently see case study 'Shotgun and Revolver Streamline Prime Focus' Global VFX Collaoration on Men In Black 3' below.

With the sequences defined, identify where the logical points to break the sequence into individual shots are. The aim of this is so that you can have animators go off and start working on shots independently of one another. Using the cuts in the animatic and previz will help you clearly define these points.

Using camera cuts will not always give you the right point to break a shot up, for example if a character is swinging around to look over her shoulder you may want to set up a camera with her facing forwards and another camera on her other side that she swings into. Classing this as one shot with two cameras will allow the animator to complete the character's animation without breaking any continuity in the animation.

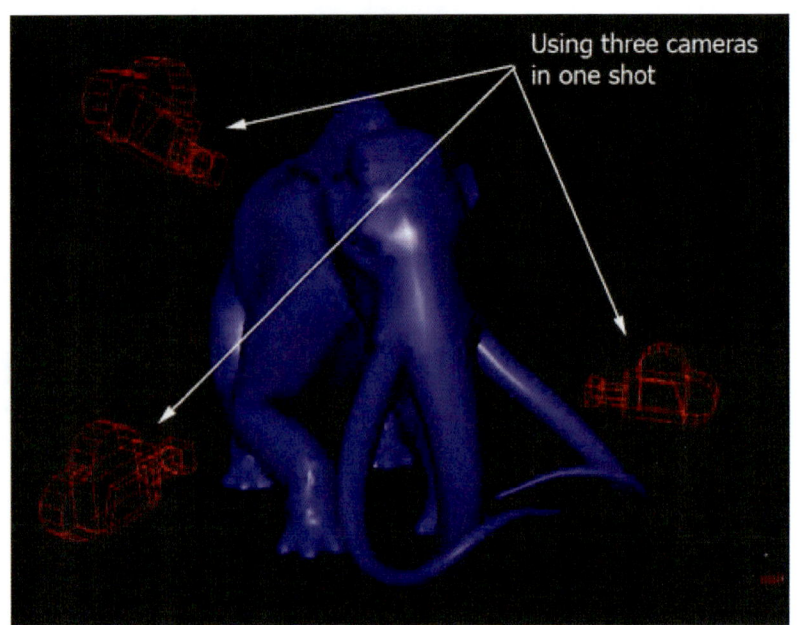

Fig 2.4 Using three cameras in one shot will allow the animator to carry on the animation with the same continuity. If you spread this out into three separate shots you would triple the work, lose continuity between shots and make any further iteration versioning more complex as you try to maintain continuity.

Now you have a shot list, start to log these somewhere, preferably in a database of some kind, there are several VFX specific databases that exists (see the next case study for an example of one). Again your budget and schedule may limit you in terms of what shot management software you can afford. Whichever route you chose you want to start logging the following

* Shot names - the name everyone will be referring to
* Shot duration - make sure people are working to the right frame lengths, this will save a lot of time and make sure people are not wasting time working on frames that are not needed
* Assets to use - make sure shots are set up to use the correct assets, props, environments and very importantly the correct camera (consider using a publishing system as we discussed above)
* Who is assigned to work on which shot - identify whose skills

VFX and CG Survival Guide for Filmmakers and Producers

can be best utilised and where
   * What iterations are the current approved assets at - e.g. which cameras to use, which model, animation etc. are the current/final versions to use.
   * Client and supervisor Feedback and its action dates - make sure everyone knows what they need to do (this is where you will enter notes from dailies)
   * Due dates - make sure everyone knows when they are expected to have the work done by. You will be truly amazed at how many producers do not let the artists know when shots/iterations are expected. Try as much as you can to keep the schedule visible. Please do not be one of those producers who storms up to an artist demanding them to hand over the shot for a client review in five minutes and please please do not be one of those producers who says that they '*needed it yesterday*', yes they exist and yes no one respects them.
   * Shot status, i.e. not started, in progress, awaiting feedback, on hold, blocked, cancelled/cut

↩	acf	Awaiting Client Feedback
👍	sgnoff	Signed Off (Client)
★	exp	exported
✂	edit	edited
✂	afe	Approved for Edit
●	apr	Director Approved
●	lap	Lead Approved
🚩	issue	Issue
🔨	revise	Revise
●	cmpt	Complete
◐	ip	In Progress
‖	hld	Hold
–	wtg	Waiting to Start
✋	nordy	Not ready to start
⊘	omt	Omit

Fig 2.5 Tracking all the possible states that a shot will identify any bottlenecks in the pipeline – you can see there are more than just 'in progress' and 'completed'. Any given shot will have to go through several departments including the all-important sign off from the

69

director/VFX supervisor. When blockages/dependencies are identified, immediate action should be taken in any downstream departments responsible.

The higher end project management software will have all these tasks integrated into a Gant chart. It will become immediately obvious if you are going to hit your deadlines, that in itself should be justification to assign some of your budget to purchase a reasonable project management tool. You of course will be tempted to catalogue this in a free spreadsheet programme, while this will get you started you will find that the spreadsheet will quickly become unwieldy for everyone to input to and managing the spread sheet will become your full time job. It will quickly become confused, misleading and a massive headache.

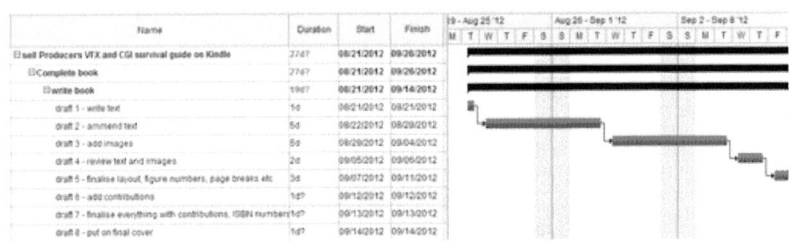

Fig 2.6 Most shot management software will also give you a Gant chart view of the project, this will show which tasks are linked/have dependencies. As artist fill in their own task status the Gant chart will auto update.

Depending upon the number of shots you have you will want to plan how your shots are going to go through the render farm. One way to have this progress smoothly is as much as you can try to get as many shots especially the layout and animation shots approved in playblast format (playblast, also known as flip booking is a sequence quickly rendered out from the application, essentially it captures the application's viewport). You should be able to get internal sign off from playblasts, more than likely you will present higher quality lit renders to the client.

Of course it depends on the complexity of the shots and how far they have progressed but generally delivering sequences to the render farm will help you progress the output further. More than likely you will experience the same rendering issues with shots in the same sequence which you can deal with at the same time. Other sequences

70

will have their own rendering issues which may require reconfiguring your render farm setups for different sequences. Also it will save you time and maximise your resources if you can have different farm setups for different requirements.

Case study 2: Shotgun and Revolver Streamline Prime Focus' Global VFX Collaboration on Men In Black 3

Case Study: June 18, 2012

Global entertainment services company Prime Focus World provides award-winning visual effects and stereo 3D conversion services to major studios around the world. Its visual effects artists have created breathtaking shots for top films such as Avatar, Tron: Legacy, and the Harry Potter, Twilight and X-Men franchises, and its stereo 3D technicians have converted blockbusters including Harry Potter and the Deathly Hallows: Part 2 and Transformers: Dark of the Moon using its proprietary 2D-to-3D process, View-D.

With facilities in the U.S., Canada, the U.K., and India, Prime Focus' Global Digital Pipeline seamlessly connects 3,000 artists and technicians worldwide and allows for around-the-clock service. In addition to adopting a more collaborative global VFX model, the company recently shifted from a Windows/3ds Max pipeline to standardizing on Maya and Nuke on Linux, and turned to infrastructure platforms like Shotgun and Revolver to evolve into the future.

"We were set to do both VFX and stereo 3D conversion on Men in Black 3," explains Prime Focus Vancouver VFX Supervisor Jon Cowley. "We already had a consistent production pipeline in place but my main concern was effective project management. When I'm supervising from Vancouver and there's a whole team in Mumbai that's working while I'm at home, or asleep – what would be the best way to manage their progress? That's when we decided to implement

Shotgun."

"Once we chose Shotgun, it was extremely easy to integrate into our pipeline – it was literally all set up over one weekend and immediately began impacting our workflow," said Cowley. Prime Focus also tapped in-house developers to spend an extra 6 weeks to integrate Shotgun into their pipeline, tailoring the software with Prime Focus-specific delivery tools and a new dailies logging system.

"We are also using the beta version of Revolver every single day and it is absolutely changing the way we work globally and will definitely become part of our standard pipeline," continued Cowley. "We're using it as a dailies review system, to give shots and annotations firsthand to all of the artists around the world."

Improved Project Management and Communication
Shotgun significantly streamlined Prime Focus' production tracking, management and overall collaboration across multiple facilities in LA, Vancouver, India and London as they delivered 319 VFX shots for MIB3. "Plates would come into Vancouver, then go to London for tracking, then to Mumbai for roto and prep, and then to LA for stereo work – so at any given time there were hundreds of versions of each shot around the world that all needed to be tracked. Shotgun allowed us to log and track everything very easily," explained Cowley.

"Shotgun was great for me as a VFX supervisor because whether I'm at work or at home, any time of day, I can always log in to review a shot and make the creative decisions I need to make based on the latest iterations," continued Cowley.

Prime Focus also developed a custom delivery tool powered by Shotgun that allowed them to easily log and track shot deliveries to the client. "That was really key for me," Cowley explained. "That tool came in very handy 3 weeks before our final deadline when the client changed a spec in our deliveries, which often happens at the 11th hour on a show. This meant we had to go back and re-deliver an entire month's worth of work – around 360 versions – of these shots. Thanks to Shotgun, one coordinator was able to easily find and re-deliver everything in a single day, whereas previously it would have taken several people several days and caused a lot of gray hairs in the process."

Looking Ahead

Prime Focus is also currently beta testing Revolver, Shotgun's new powerful all-in-one review product. Revolver combines production tracking and review, making it easy for teams in any location to view the latest work in the context of the cut, browse and compare iterations, annotate on images, write notes, and collaborate on work in real-time. Tweak's high-end native player, RV, is integrated to provide real-time playback of hi-res frames from local storage at the desktop or in the screening room.

"My background is in industrial engineering, which is all about how to make products more efficient," said Cowley. "Revolver does exactly that. It allows us to dramatically decrease the time between when the VFX supervisor reviews a shot and when notes on that shot get back to the artist. Now I can be looking at a shot and annotating it in real-time during dailies review, and before I even leave dailies I know that my notes are already being addressed by the artist. The size of that gap is what can make or break a deadline – so the immediate feedback that Revolver provides is really invaluable."

Shotgun and Revolver ultimately allowed for smoother and faster project management and delivery on Prime Focus' MIB3 VFX pipeline, positively impacting their 200 artists worldwide who worked on the film. Prime Focus is currently working on visual effects for Total Recall and other upcoming feature films, building their workflow around a Shotgun and Revolver core.

To learn more about Revolver, watch the video tour, or sign-up for updates and the private beta, please visit http://www.shotgunsoftware.com/revolver

About Shotgun Software

Shotgun Software was founded in 2006 by a group of visual effects professionals to build production tracking and pipeline solutions. The founding members worked together on a major studio animated feature and developed Shotgun to fill the mounting industry need for a commercially viable system for managing complex projects spread across multiple locations. Shotgun has more than 350 animation, visual effects and game development clients including Digital Domain, Double Negative, Reliance, Framestore, Pixomondo, Playstation, Blizzard and Zoic Studios. For more information and an online demonstration visit http://www.shotgunsoftware.com

About Prime Focus World

Acknowledged as a preeminent source of creative and technical services for the global entertainment industry, Prime Focus World provides visual effects and stereo 3D conversion to major studios and filmmakers around the world. Prime Focus has brought its 3D conversion expertise to top-tier Hollywood movies including Star Wars: Episode One – The Phantom Menace, Harry Potter and the Deathly Hallows: Part 2, Narnia: The Voyage of the Dawn Treader, Shrek, Green Lantern, Immortals and Transformers: Dark of the Moon. In addition, Prime Focus has created breathtaking visual effects for the Academy Award winning film Avatar, for the blockbuster Harry Potter, Twilight Saga and X-Men franchises; and for global releases including Tron: Legacy, The A-Team, Sucker Punch, Unknown and the 2011 Palme d'Or winning Tree of Life. Headquartered in Los Angeles, Prime Focus has world-class facilities in the United States, Canada, the U.K., and India.

For more information on Prime Focus worldwide, please visit www.primefocusworld.com.

Case study courtesy of Shotgun software: http://www.shotgunsoftware.com

VFX and CG Survival Guide for Filmmakers and Producers

Case Study 3: Integrating CGI and VFX into live action

When you start putting in CG elements into live action you are going to come across a new set of issues at the start and end of your pipeline. The stages mentioned in case 1 will all be relevant, think of them as the meat in the sandwich, you are now going to add a layer either side. At the start is the process of preparing the film footage to go into the CG pipeline, at the end is a process of compositing the rendered frames onto the live action footage.

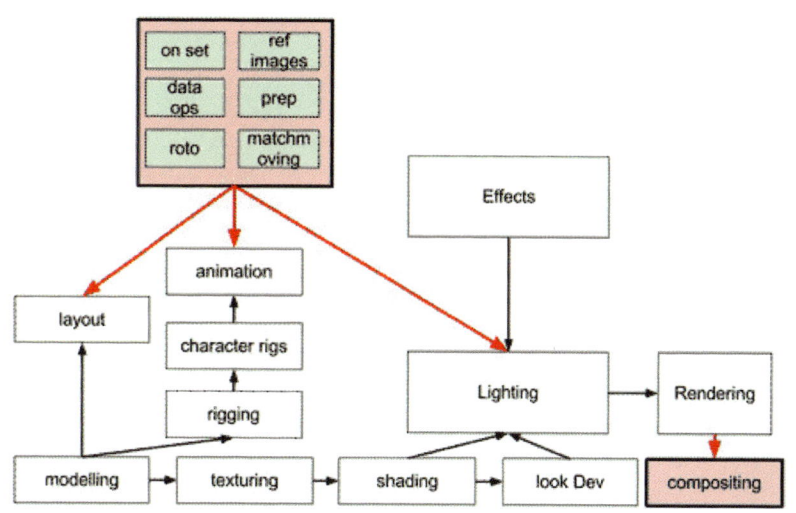

Fig 2.7 Adding live action plates adds tasks to the start and end of the VFX/CG pipeline and creates new interrelationships.

75

Preparing film/video to go into the process

Firstly you are going to have to store all the frames (depending upon your format you will either have 24 frames per second, 25 frames per second or 30 frames per second) onto you server and make them accessible to your artists. Different artists will require different quality of frames, those artists who are concerned with precise integration tasks (roto artists, matchmovers, lighting TDs and compositors) will need higher quality frames while other artists (animators, effects artists) will not need such high quality frames to work with.

The choice comes down to a matter of playback speed versus accuracy.

What happens is that the software (whether 3D or 2D) will have to load the image sequence into memory or read it off disc, obviously the higher quality the image is the bigger its file size will be. Bigger file sizes in turn mean the slower it takes to advance through the timeline. It is advantageous for animators and effects artists to be able to playback through the timeline at reasonable speed (to see their animation/simulation working in near real-time), other artists such as lighters are more generally interested in the still frame and therefore value precision ahead of speed. The moving images from animation and effects would have been seen and approved before they get to the lighters. The onus now is on the quality of the lighting and rendering integration where you need higher quality backplates to composite against than you needed in either animation or effects.

Once you have the footage accessible on your system the first group of people who will need access to them is the roto, prep and matchmove departments. They will each prepare the footage so that it can be passed onto the rest of the CG team.

Roto is short for rotoscoping - a process whereby amongst others, removal of non-filmed elements such as wires, markers, cross hairs etc are removed from the film frame. In other cases it could be where actors are separated from backgrounds, or certain props are separated from others. The aim being that you want to create an image with several channels, one of the channels would be your actors, one perhaps your environment, ultimately one of the channels is to be left blank, this blank channel is where your CG and VFX is going to go in, i.e. the output from the middle process.

Prep, short for preparation is any other tasks that need to be done like

- removing bits of dust from that may have come onto the frame,
- repair any scratches (especially from film reels) or other artifacts,
- have the frame put into a particular format such as any lower quality frames e.g. jpgs with a transparent background for the animators and effects artists,
- flattening the plate - a camera lens like a human eye has a degree of curvature, flattening is the process where you would un-distort the curvature on the plate and give it to the artist to create their CG. The perfectly flat rendered output of the CG will then go through a process where it is distorted to match up again with the original distortion inherent in the original frame.

Matchmoving as we discussed in part 1 is the process where a virtual camera is created that matches the real world camera. It is a very in-depth subject but essentially think of it like this, if you have a camera moving through a room and you want to add a CG sculpture into the room. Your lighting artist is going to need a camera to render out the sculpture and all its shadows, reflections etc. from otherwise the rendered sculpture will have a different perspective from everything else in the room. Add to that a moving camera and you can see how quickly your sculpture would be sliding all over the background image. Take this analogy further and have a moving character interacting with real world elements. Without a virtual camera how is your animator to know where the elements are to animate the character against?

It is the role of matchmoving to provide a camera for all the other artists to work with. There are a number of considerations involved in matchmoving, but for you, the producer, you need to know that before any 'meaningful' production work can begin on a given shot, the shot itself will need to be matchmoved and a camera needs to be output and passed across. You can of course have other tasks run alongside this, for instance a character rig, look development set up, R&D on a new crowd system does not need to be stopped while a camera is being prepared. Try to schedule all these pre-production tasks to come to an end at the same time that the cameras are to be delivered from matchmove.

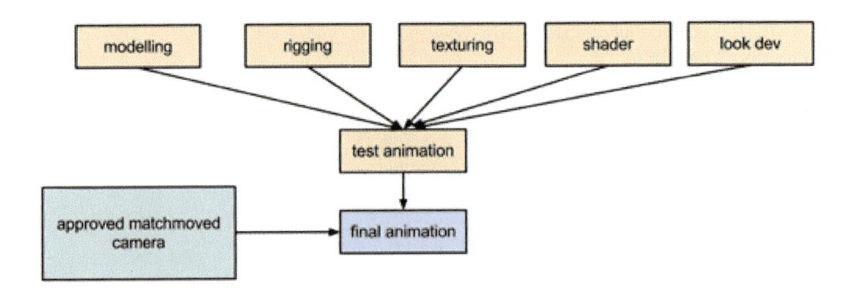

VFX and CG Survival Guide for Filmmakers and Producers

```
[modelling]  [rigging]  [texturing]  [shader]  [look dev]
                        ↓
                 [test animation]
                        ↓
[approved matchmoved camera] → [final animation]
```

Fig 2.7 a lot of preparation work can go on while matchmoving is being done, but no final animation would be able to be output until a matchmoved camera is approved

Also realise that not all the cameras need to be matchmoved before the production tasks need to begin. Oftentimes you will be receiving footage in phases from the client, you can start working on some shots with cameras while delaying other production tasks on other shots while those cameras and footage are being prepared.

Final word on matchmoving for you to know is to have a solid accurate sign off process that the cameras have been matched properly. If you do not then you are going to be wasting a lot of artist's time and effort working on their tasks only to find that the CG and live action does not sit properly when composited at the final stage. You'll have to go back and redo the camera, which in turn may mean that every other production task may need to be redone and re-rendered.

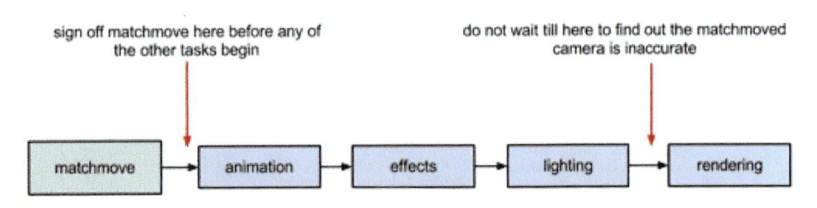

```
sign off matchmove here before any of          do not wait till here to find out the matchmoved
     the other tasks begin                              camera is inaccurate
             ↓                                                    ↓
[matchmove] → [animation] → [effects] → [lighting] → [rendering]
```

Fig 2.8 do not be tempted to provide temporary cameras so you can get downstream departments working while you wait for matchmoved cameras to be approved. You will find that a lot or rework will be required if the camera is inaccurate

On the other end of the pipeline is a stage called compositing, this is where a compositor will take the film footage and integrate it with the rendered CG that has come out of your render farm. Here again you as a producer need to identify all the elements that will be coming out of the CG department (e.g. a monster, a building, a car, dust, smoke, sparks, a typhoon) that need to be composited back onto the backplate. You need to schedule work such that these elements are delivered by a whole host of artists to the compositor at a roughly the same time. Treat each element as a *dependency*, you can not have the final image until all these elements (dependencies for the compositor) have been finished and signed off. Remember always that these CG elements all have their own multiple dependencies as well.

Case study 4: CG in computer games - adding programmers, designers and QA into the mix

So we've seen a lot of the processes involved in CG, now consider the added complexity when all this CG needs to be interactive with a player instead of a viewer.

In the world of computer games you may be mistaken for thinking that the CG visuals will take priority over everything else and that design and programming would be subservient to graphics. In reality this is seldom the case. Best case scenario is that all three disciplines would be equally prioritised. But you will find that design will lead the way, programming will say what is possible and art will have to strike the best balance between what design want and what programming can deliver.

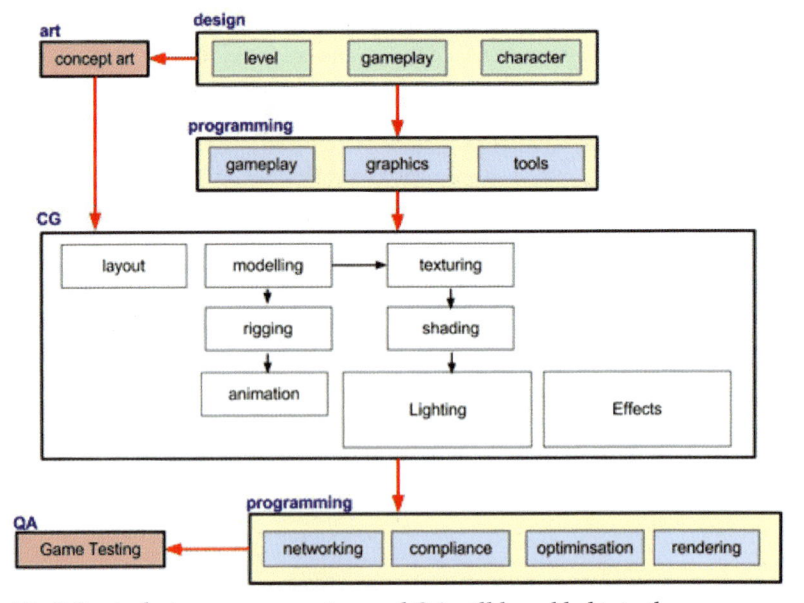

VFX and CG Survival Guide for Filmmakers and Producers

Fig 2.9 art, design, programming and QA will be added into the base CG pipeline, note i. in some teams the CG and art team will merge into one ii. effects and lighting are no longer linked and can progress in parallel, iii. your CG teams are now dependent upon design being finalled and programming fully functional both before and after work enters and leaves the CG department

The CG department in computer games companies may be referred to as a part of the 'Art Department', which will also comprises concept art. From there the art department will then closely resemble that of a film or TV CG department with more specialised departments of environment, character, level design (equivalent of layout), effects, lighting and GUI (graphical user interface - typically where you score, status and any directional maps are displayed over the top of the game). There is an added role of the technical artist whose job it is to link all the graphics into the various programming constructs of the game engine, which could include rigging characters and having certain triggers in the game to activate particular animations.

The graphics will then be linked back into the game in a defined way that corresponds with the game engine. The basic approach is to check-in an element into the game's database and have the game refer to the particular element through a declaration which points to the

VFX and CG Survival Guide for Filmmakers and Producers

element to insert when it is needed, for instance only play the grenade explosion when a grenade is thrown (otherwise you will have a very peculiar game indeed).

```
┌─────────────────┐      ┌─────────────────────┐
│ particle system │─────▶│ particle system     │
│ created in editor│     │ checked into game   │
└─────────────────┘      │ database            │
                         └─────────────────────┘
                                   ▲
                                   │                      ┌──────────────┐
                                   │      the game will   │   event is   │
                         ┌─────────────────┐ look for the │ triggered in │
                         │ a declaration   │ declaration  │    game      │
                         │ points to this  │◀─────────────│              │
                         │ particle system │ to tell it   │              │
                         │                 │ which particle│              │
                         └─────────────────┘ system to play└──────────────┘
```

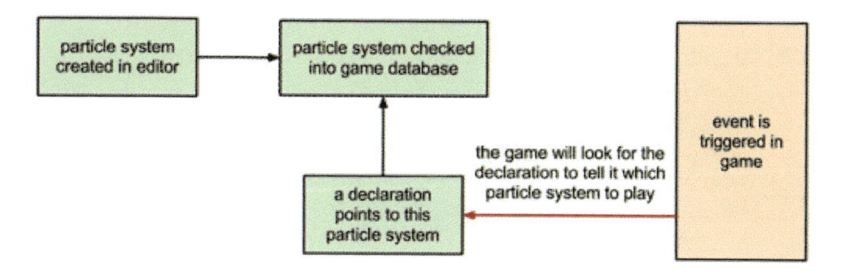

Fig 2.10 the declaration is what links the particle system to the trigger in game. The declaration can point to any number of different particle systems and can also call sound and light effects too.

From your perspective as a producer your considerations are to identify what design want in the game and how programming and art can deliver that. On the surface it might sound reasonably straight forward but a game is seldom created in a vacuum. Game design is an iterative process and one that is subject to change. Game designers can only really assess how well a design feature works when it is implemented and tested fully. This of course means that game pieces have to be built and delivered for a true assessment to take place.

The relationship between programming and art will depend upon how well the code or art is already developed. For many franchises the code and art will already have been established, studios that develop continuous racing and sports games franchises have been doing so for many generations of the game. The code and art are fairly well locked down, the gameplay changes are to do with having the latest cars (or cars that were not in the previous games), new tracks, or in the case of sports games having the correct players for the correct clubs.

For studios that are developing a new game or inheriting a franchise from another studio the link between art and programming will be a lot more complex. It will involve what assets are already in place and what needs to be built. From an art side this would include all the usual suspects of props, characters and effects, from the programming side it would include what pieces of code persists and can be reused and what needs to be written from scratch.

Your job as a producer will be to sync deliveries of gameplay and art that can be imported into the game together so the design of the game can be tested. For example the player has to repair a crane as a gameplay objective which then kicks off a spectacular shower of sparks which opens a gate leading into the next level of the game. For this to work the crane and the gate have to be modelled. To test the sparks on the opening of the gate some code must be written that will trigger the sparks to play and code needs to be written that will trigger the animation of the opening of the gate which in turn will need code written to transport the player into the new level.

Another department that needs to be involved is that of Quality Assurance (QA) otherwise known as game testers whose job it is to test the gameplay elements of the game. Their feedback will then go back into the design, programming and art departments and often will create a change list that will require you to reschedule work for departments who are already in the process of delivering other items from the release list.

The use of AGILE and SPRINT in game is more prevalent than in film or TV. A game brief is subject to far more change than either film or TV and has many more technical constraints. In film, a reel of film or hard disc containing the final images will be played back through projector and the frame rate (frames may be played back at 24, 25, 30 or 60 frames per second - check with your technical team) will never drop. You can then make a shot as complex and detailed as you like and send it to a render farm and wait for it to be rendered - in game this luxury does not exists.

A single frame of game may run on a games console (be it a XBox or PlayStation) or a smart phone and as such all the processing of the gameplay, programming and art all has to be processed by the internal memory of the device. You can see to run a game at a reasonable frame rate (in games a higher frame rate is aimed for than in film, a frame rate of 30 will provide acceptable playback speeds, although your target frame rate may be 60 frames per seconds) all the elements going in have to be calculated very quickly.

The challenges for you as a producer will differ greatly, whereas you may think of film as a relatively linear workflow with games you will need to keep on top of your schedule and identify any dependencies, risks or impediments very early on otherwise you will not be hitting your milestones and the workload will very quickly spiral out of control. Even if you do hit the milestones, work may have to flow back if QA (Quality Assurance - also known as game testers) find that the games slows downs/lags in certain areas and frame rates are too slow or the game crashes at a particular point. QA will find the flaws in the game that design and scheduling will not be able to account for. Build in a set period of contingency between each milestone.

Be sure to keep on top of meetings and reviews. Working between departments and having clear definitions of work to be done is imperative, what is a low priority item for the programming department may be impeding an artist from being able to start/complete their task list. The programmer may not appreciate that their work is directly supporting an artist to complete theirs. These dependencies need a lead time for the programmer to test that the artists will be able to progress without any delay.

The use of placeholders is very useful. The idea that an artist can make a very simple placeholder and test that it will play at the right point in the game, for instance an explosion is defined by gameplay to happen when a box (of cookies) is opened. For the effects artist to create an exploding cookie box he/she needs some way to see the resultant explosion in game, i.e. they need a way to trigger the effect in game.

A simple placeholder sprite (a sprite is a graphic which always faces the camera like a flat plane, for instance the sprite in this example could be a flat card facing the camera with the word 'kapow') could be checked into the game. The programmer could then wire up all the events in game that would lead to the explosion. If the programmer can then open the box and see the 'kapow' placeholder sprite then they should be able to see the final explosion when the effects are completed. The effect artist can then start and iterate on the effect replacing the 'kapow' placeholder with their effect. If however this programming construct is not in place then the effects artist will be blocked and cannot start to implement the effect. Asking the programmer to then build the construct will not only disrupt their work schedule (which will cause further delays down the line) it will waste the effects artist's time and create a backlog of work in that department.

You as a producer are the one who has to make sure all such

blockages and dependencies are resolved, use the QA team here to check all gameplay elements will trigger the right events through the use of simple placeholders.

Part 3: Producer Practicalities

Weapon of choice - working on multiple software in the same show

There is a myriad of different 3D and 2D software packages out there, some of which promise to be the best most complete all round package, others claim to be the most specialised at what they do. The aim of this chapter is to explain to you why and when you may choose to blend different packages together and what the implications of doing so are.

If you are putting together CGI/VFX together with live footage you are going to need to have the following

- an image prep package
- matchmoving software
- modelling software
- rigging software
- texturing software
- UV layout software

- animation software
- effects software
- lighting software
- rendering management tools

- compositing software
- shot management/tracking software

You can see already from the list of things you need you are going to be spending a lot of money on software licences, bear in mind each artist will need their own copy of that particular software and in terms of rendering on a farm, each software will need a render token or licence to be installed on each blade of the farm.

This is where the decision to purchase an all-round software that can do it all or whether to go down the route of buying specialised software for each task has to be made. You will also want to take a similar view of the artists you hire, whether to hire a generalist who could do a reasonable job across the different tasks or to hire specialists for a particular task. Both approaches have various merits.

So why has the 3D software package disseminated into such a wide array of packages? Why has a split been formed between specialised packages and more general ones? And most importantly for you which route do you choose to go down?

In terms of your decision making do you want really fine control and efficiency over each specific aspect of the process? For instance you can model reasonably well in an all singing all dancing 3D package. But you can get even finer control in a dedicated modelling package such as ZBrush or Mudbox, these are also known as sculpting packages because they go beyond modelling and allow the artist to sculpt - something which is not included in a more general 3D package - which as well as having modelling tools will also have animation, lighting and effects tools built in.

Again the same is true of many other areas of the pipeline, there are specialised tools for UV layout which will allow your artist to layout UVs faster and with more control. There are specialised effects packages that deal specifically with fluid simulation. Perhaps if your show is fluid sim heavy you may want to look into this. The key is to identify your requirements early in the process; story boards, animatics and previz will help you here.

Bear in mind each of these packages will need a way to be integrated back into your pipeline and input/output information needs to be passed from one format into another.

Your main decision will be based on how specialised your requirements are. If you are required to insert a hard edged model (like a prop) into a shot that will be seen from a distance away, you perhaps do not need to invest in specialised packages and can use a more general one. If however you are going to have close up shots of a sea monster throwing water against a ship you probably should start to look at the advanced fluid simulation packages.

These specialised packages will do just what 'they say on the tin', i.e. a fluid simulation package will only do a fluid simulation, it will do it very well and efficiently with preciser controls than a more general 3D package will, but you will need to take that simulation into another package to texture, shade, light and render. Therefore you can see that you are going to need an all round package that can gather all your simulations, animations, models, rigs etc. so that you can light and render the final frames out. This core software package will be the central hub that any other specialist solutions will feed into. So you may ask 'if I'm already spending all this money on a 3D package why should I be spending extra money on specialist packages?' and you would be right to ask that.

The truth is that the host package can do everything but a obviously a package that focuses on one specific area will be able to do that specific task better than a package that tries to provide a catch all.

Specialist packages exist and are being developed for almost every part of the pipeline. These packages have come about due to a demand/need to do a specific task faster and with more control. If you are on a long-form project investing in these may ultimately save you time and money over the course of the show. Consider looking into these, there are even advanced lighting tools that allow you to design and implement light setups in a fraction of the time than it would in the 3D host programme. Calculate whether the efficiency increases outweigh the extra costs of these packages and how you will implement it back into the pipeline.

Working late nights + weekends != good producer

So it happens, milestones are missed, dependencies are ignored, due dates are not communicated, projects spiral out of control. More often than not, it is the artists who rescue the project. But does this have to be the case? The reason this happens is that basic principles are not practiced and lessons are not learnt. The VFX industry is reaching a point of maturity now whereby artists are not willing to work late nights and weekends when producers are not putting together feasible schedules and refusing to acknowledge mistakes. When the industry was in its infancy, there was a certain amount of goodwill afforded to producers as everyone in the industry was on a learning curve - that time has now passed.

You as a producer should take responsibility for projects falling behind schedule, in fact the best producers do. They constantly check in with artists and have a two way communication channel. The concept of dailies is really important, this is where you gather everyone involved in the project to see the latest outputs. Whether or not a particular artist has anything ready to show they should all attend.

An extension to dailies is desk rounds, this is where the VFX supervisor and an production coordination (also known as an associate producer – an honorary title a production coordinator will take in lieu of a raise) go round every artists desks to check in and see how a shot is progressing, whether they need any direction or help, if there is anything impeding their progress and when you can expect to see an output. It is also a way for you to amend the schedule if someone is falling behind (or getting ahead) of their schedule. This is also known as a 'fail fast' approach, that is to keep the hierarchy relatively flat and allow artists to present work often and in various stages of development. You can then pick up on any potential problems a lot faster in the process.

Do not just present a schedule to your artists and expect them to deliver on those days. This is riddled with problems, namely if they do deliver on that date, will they have delivered what the client expects to see? By having desk rounds the VFX supervisor and artist can iterate on a daily basis and make sure the particular asset has all the feedback incorporated into it before the final delivery is due.

Chart your progress in terms of a burndown chart, this is where you have a complete list of things that need to be done, each time one item is done have it removed from the list so the total number of tasks is updated. You can then measure the 'to do list' versus with the 'days to delivery' number to calculate how many tasks need to be completed each day.

Remember due to the pipelined nature of the work, any delays in downstream departments will filter through to upstream departments. In practice a delay of a day from getting the final rig and character to animation would mean that animation is delayed. That in turn could provide a two day delay to get the animation passed onto lighting, which in turn could add another two day delay to get the images rendered and passed to compositing. You can see now that what started as a one day delay for rigging has now meant that compositing are now five days behind their schedule before even getting any elements to start working on.

Worked Example – a bear walks into a bar

Here is a worked example to show a more complicated chain of delays and why you need to be on top of this from the start.

This is a simple two shot sequence

    shot 1 - bear walks into a bar
    shot 2 - bear sits down on bar stool

This is how you have scheduled the shot to deliver to clients

August		TASK	START DATE	DUE DATE	TOTAL (days)	ASSIGNEE
1	Mon	Bear model to be made	1st Aug	5th Aug	5	Modeller
		Hair and Fur tests	1st Aug	5th Aug	5	FX Artist
2	Tue					
3	Wed	Bear rig to be made	3rd Aug	5th Aug	2	Rigger
		Light tests	3rd Aug	5th Aug	2	Generalist
4	Thu					
5	Fri					
6	Sat					
7	Sun					
8	Mon	Shot 1: Animation	8th Aug	10th Aug	3	Animator
9	Tue					
10	Wed					
11	Thu	Shot 2: Animation	11th Aug	12th Aug	2	Animator
12	Fri					
13	Sat					
14	Sun					
15	Mon	shot 1: Lighting	15th Aug	16th Aug	2	Lighter
		shot 1: FX	15th Aug	16th Aug	2	FX Artist
16	Tue	shot 1: Rendering	16th Aug	17th Aug	2	Rendering
17	Wed	shot 2: Lighting	17th Aug	18th Aug	2	Lighter
		shot 1: Compositing	17th Aug	19th Aug	2	Compositor
18	Thu					
19	Fri	shot 2: Rendering	19th Aug	19th Aug	1	Rendering
20	Sat					
21	Sun					
22	Mon	shot 2: Compositing	22nd Aug	23rd Aug	2	Compositor
23	Tue					
24	Wed	Conform + delivery	24th Aug	24th Aug	1	Conform
25	Thu	DELIVERY	25th Aug	25th Aug	1	Production
26	Fri					

Fig 3.1 Scheduling two shots with delivery dates for all teams, hard delivery on the 25th August

So you present this schedule to the artists and leave them to get on with it.

Error: you do not do dailies or desk rounds

In week 1 the modeller models the bear and delivers it on time, your VFX supervisor looks at it, does not like it, the ears are too big, the snout is too deep, etc. The modeller has to go back and change it. Now your animator doesn't have a model to start animating, he/she is delayed by two days waiting for the model to be finished.

Shot 1 Animation now begins on 10th August; the animator rushes and works late nights to hit their delivery for the end of the week. The supervisor looks at the animation at the end of the week, it is not good enough, too many mistakes clearly the work of a stressed, over stretched and tired animator. It is not going to be good enough for the client. It has to be redone.

You force the animator to work the weekend to correct it. Monday morning comes, still it is not good enough, more tweaks need to be done to get it to standard. It is delivered two days later on the 17th Aug. Now the fur takes as long as it takes to simulate, you cannot make the computer calculate it any faster, the FX team is not going to hit the target to pass it to lighting. The lighter now gets it two days late, they light it as fast as they can.

Again another bottleneck is the rendering - the frames take as long as they take to render, you cannot make them go any faster. By the time the frames are delivered to the compositor, it is now the date that it should have been booked in for the conform. The conform will most likely be done at a separate facility that you had previously booked in. You phone them to rearrange a time for two days later than scheduled, at the same time you had better phone the client and tell them that they will not be taking delivery as agreed.

You can see from this simple example how checking in through dailies and desk rounds would have saved you so much time, even working late nights and weekends could not save the project, if anything that time was wasted as you had a tired, stressed out, unhappy team of artists.

If you had started with desk rounds you would have been able to identify that the ears were too big and the snout was too deep from day one. The modeller could have fixed it and any other items early on in the process. Again same holds true with the animator, checking in with them earlier you could have fed back on how the bear needs to 'look around' before finding his seat, that the bear 'needs to lean forward' when sitting down etc. This fail fast process means that artists can get to the right results without pouring in time and effort in going off in the wrong direction.

It is not the fault of the individual artist, all these items are subject to individual interpretation – art is ultimately a subjective medium. You as a producer need to be constantly checking in and making sure the artists are receiving the correct direction and feedback. After all you have hired *artists* and not *mind readers*. It is your job to check and get feedback to make sure they are outputting what is expected otherwise you will start slipping behind schedule very fast.

Now imagine extending that into a five shot sequence of

shot 1 - bear walks into a bar
shot 2 - bear sits down on bar stool
shot 3 - bear orders a beer
shot 4 - close up of the beer
shot 5 - close up of a satisfied bear nodding knowingly to camera

Even with a schedule this is going to be delayed massively if you do not keep checking in. You can see now how important those shot tracking softwares are (try monitoring all this in your excel worksheet).

Part 4: Low/No Budget VFX

Can low/no Budget filmmaking still have VFX?

The short answer to this chapter is yes, not only yes, but the effects themselves do not have to be second rate either. This chapter is going to be about what you can do as a producer to make sure every penny spent on VFX is maximised and efficient.

Plan

The more planning up front on a shot that you do will allow you to both see any potential issues that may occur and allow you to progress smoother through the shoot. From a VFX viewpoint you will want to produce as much concept art for the particular VFX that you need. It is much more cost effective to work up and develop any VFX in preproduction.

VFX and CG Survival Guide for Filmmakers and Producers

Shot 1

Shot 2

Shot 3

Fig 4.1 Effects can be shown in concept art at an early stage helping you to cost the show and have effects previz done cheaply up front before shot production begins and time constraints kick in. Concept Art from Digitopia: Discover Me – director: Farhan Qureshi, Artist: Stephen Trumble, © Farhan Qureshi 2010

Have several iterations of concept art so you can fine tune the particular VFX, whether it be a CG monster or a tornado, the concept art will show you what elements you could do on set and what you would need to do in CG. Money spent in developing the concept art into story boards and previz will lessen your exposure to escalating post production costs.

Share all of this concept art with the post production facility or artists that you hire to do the VFX. They will be able to make suggestions on how to build the VFX, what precautions you need to consider on set and what information they will need during the shoot to efficiently carry out the VFX.

- measure the set for matchmove and lighting
- take reference photos for texturing and lighting
- where and when to have moving cameras
- how to position foreground elements to mask and set extension work

Taking a VFX supervisor on set

On set money spent on hiring a VFX supervisor is well spent and will save you money further down the line. If the VFX supervisor is the one from the facility who will eventually carry out the VFX, he/she will be able to make sure any data they recorded can instantly be transferred back to the facility enabling them to start preparing for when you deliver the plates.

Generally the on set VFX supervisor will record the data required by the matchmove and lighting departments. If you have moving cameras they will need to be tracked, adding an extra phase to the VFX. Obviously by keeping the camera stationary during the VFX shots will largely eliminate/simplify the matchmove process – a small amount of matchmove may still be required to line up the virtual camera to the real camera, but the onset VFX supervisor should ensure the camera data is recorded (camera height, distance from object, focal length, tilt angles etc.) thus keeping the matchmove process straight forward enough.

Whether the camera is moving or not make sure that there are obvious features to track on the set, e.g. if you are unable to put up red tracking markers on a green/blue screen then make sure the set has some distinctive features on it that could be used as tracking guides – this will also save time and money on having to clean up any extra tracking markers that you would have to otherwise paint out in post-production.

In the case of a CG character that needs to be added you may find it will save time to avoid showing its contact point with the ground in shot, i.e. showing its feet touching the floor. This is basically a quick way to save the additional element of tracking. Often on especially low/no budget productions you may not be able to get good enough tracking data to the matchmove department – really if you are working at such a low/no budget you would not be able to afford the added phase of matchmove – therefore composing the shots whereby you are not showing the CG character's feet, will avoid seeing its feet slipping on set. The animator can then roughly animate the character's position to keep it relative still. Not an ideal solution but I am showing you workarounds that you will need to consider and discuss with your VFX facility or artists that you will hire. The more of these you can get an agreement on earlier the more time and money you will save later.

Set extensions is another common area where low budget films can appear to have higher production values than otherwise. If you are planning of having set extensions done, use the VFX supervisor to advise and suggest solutions to where and how practical elements could be arranged to allow for seamless insertion of the virtual elements. They will take as many reference photos as they can to capture materials and textures to ensure the set extensions match correctly.

The biggest challenge of adding virtual smoke effects which are impractical to shoot on the day will be that of compositing the effects onto the plate, especially around moving characters and objects. Consider how much movement will be in the plate, as this will potentially add a lot of work for the roto depatments. Generally if you can film real smoke in the scene this is better and will save you more money than adding CG smoke, however health and safety laws may limited the amount of real effects you can add.

In post

The more iterations on one shot that you do means that there is less time available for other shots. Always look at the big picture, if you have a hundred VFX shots to do then identify which are your money shots, which are the ones that will hold in the audience's memory?

It is helpful for you to think in terms of breaking your shots into A, B and C grade shots. Of course every shot is an A grade shot, otherwise why would it be in the movie? Put it this way, an A grade shot is one where the effects are to the fore, where the effects are more complicated, where if it was done wrong it would break the viewer's involvement in the story. C grade shots are ones in which, in the extreme case if you had effects missing would it break the flow of the story?

If you are unable to categorise any of your shots as A, B or C then rank them in order. This you should be able to do, the top third of shots are now your A grade shots, the middle third your B grade and the final third your C grade shots.

Now you have categorised your shots start budgeting time and resources to these. Do not spend the same amount of time and resources on a grade C shot as you would on a grade A shot. Give the A grade shots priority, push them ahead in the schedule if you can. Have the facility present these first so you can take your time to assess and give feedback on them. While you assess them, the studio/artists can progress with the B grade ones.

Being flexible on the on the C grade shots, will allow more time for the A grade shots.

While allowing time up front for planning, previz and carrying out the initial animation or effect will produce a better result, the real quality improvements come from carrying out iterations. Generally the more iterations of a shot the better the shot will be. By watching the shot evolve you can fine tune it by iterating further. However this comes with a caution and the concept of diminishing returns comes in, so do not over iterate – move onto the next shot and come back to this later if time permits.

Remember you are on a budget and the facility is already doing you a favour by doing the work at a lower rate. This will become even more apparent when you are hiring freelance artists for a lower price or even for free. Now you are relying on their goodwill to get the shots done. Even though you have thoughts and feedback over their work, pushing for too many iterations will see them lose interest and just want to get through the shots. You do not want them to rush through the shots or worse yet lose interest and not complete the job. One way to achieve better results when working with people for free is to have them lead the development and throughput by allowing them to assess and sign off their own shots. By giving them the responsibility in this area they will want to put forward the best work they can.

Make sure there is something in it for them as well. The key to getting favours done is to bear in mind the phrase 'what's in it for me, what's in it for them?'. There has to be a compelling reasons they want to work for free, either they really believe in the project, which is what they will tell you, the truth is they either need to prove themselves or need to build a reel to get a job in VFX. It is highly unlikely you will get an Oscar nominated animator from Aardman or Pixar to work on your movie for free. You will be getting students, or more likely runners who want to work their way upwards. While they are willing to work hard and long hours they are going to have gaps in their knowledge and skill base compared to more accomplished artists. Bear that in mind when reviewing their work, what they lack in speed and finesse though they will more than make up with in commitment and enthusiasm. Be wary of wearing out either of these two by giving excessive feedback, instead encourage them to self critique their work - ultimately they are looking to put these shots on their showreels. You will find they will come up with far better and more accurate feedback than you will. They will also come up with better solutions to improve their work and largely manage their own workflows and schedules. There will be very little need to micromanage them at this stage.

Part 5: Conclusion

How to be a good producer

Communicate – dailies are the preferred method

The ways to communicate are constantly growing. The method that has served best in VFX is 'dailies'. This is where the various teams meet, preferably in the morning, to see the latest states of the shots. This can be done on a department by department basis, i.e. have effects dailies, lighting dailies, animation dailies or it can be done on a sequence by sequence basis where you have animators, lighters, effects artists, compositors, who are working on the same shot, all in the same session.

Generally on a heavily pipelined show, one in which assets are passed between departments without much interaction between them, you may prefer to do department dailies. Using your shot management software you can have artists update their shot status to 'in dailies' this will automatically trigger an email to production to upload the latest version to dailies.

Whether you choose to invite all the artists in the department or just those whose shots are ready to be viewed will depend upon the overall progression of the project. It is better to ensure the whole department is present for dailies as, for example, the effects artists or animators will learn from feedback for one particular shot and can factor that feedback in when they have a similar shot or the VFX supervisor can explain the look of a whole sequence (as you will generally be dealing in sequences) to the artists collectively and as a group the direction can be established. This will of course save masses of time further down the line.

There are times when some artists will not be able to attend due to time constraints and pressure to meet deadlines. As a producer you should see this is as a false economy as a twenty minutes daily session where all the artists can glean something, will help all of them with their shots.

Generally you will want to ensure outputs for dailies are in as close to final version for the particular discipline as they can be, but as we will see below (in desk rounds) there are other ways to get the shot closer to its final status by intervening earlier.

In dailies make copious notes and do not be afraid to ask the VFX supervisor/animation director to slow down so you can write this all up. Miscommunication through a 'follow up e-mail' or schedule is more time consuming than asking everyone to pause for a few seconds. Especially when the e-mail lands in someone's inbox who was not at that dailies session.

Try to keep dailies focused on each shot at a time and avoid conversations going off in tangents – summarise the feedback at the end to make sure everyone understands what it is they need to do.

Doing dailies in the morning gives everyone a target to work to by the end of the day. Also the likelihood of fire fighting and emergency meetings is less in the morning than later in the day. Morning dailies also helps to get everyone in on time.

When working with satellite/remote artists across the world use whatever networking/web conferencing facilities you have available to have them sit in on dailies.

In games it is a bit more difficult to have dailies as there is no formal way of viewing each event sequentially. You will probably have to replace the concept of dailies with game tests or screen capturing the part in game. Either way getting feedback to the artists and having that feedback added to their schedule is vitally important.

To assess the element you will have to go to that part of the game which you will spend a long time just to reach. Have your programmers/designers write scripts that will take you straight to that part of the game or trigger that cutscene/effect from wherever you are in the game.

Structure

You know how the CG/VFX pipeline works and how the different elements feed into one another. You will need to balance out the workflow to avoid departments having 'nothing' to do while others are 'overwhelmed' with work.

Identify your bottlenecks early, sometimes these bottlenecks will shift as you discover that you may have underestimated a particular part or the intended solution does not work for a particular problem. Be prepared to change the structure to cope, shift priorities and resources as necessary but be careful not to isolate departments/people for the sake of servicing others. Not only will this create disharmony but essentially teams that are having problems/not meeting their deadlines will be the ones that require more resources - while teams that have performed well will suffer as a consequence. This obviously sends out the wrong message so make sure that any shifts in resources and priorities are balanced out as soon as possible.

Structure your projects to allow for technical challenges; these will occur in the most complex areas of the projects. Look at the animation, are there areas of particularly challenging animation, is the rig set up to handle the range of animation that is being asked of it? Are your effects solutions suitable, do you have a proven pipeline that can produce the effects you are after?

Use previz and prototyping time at the start of the project to test out your effects while modelling, texturing etc. are all in progress. Use your look development time to test out different render settings, track the quality of the renders with the time it takes to render. Measure what all the extra high quality settings give you in terms of time taken to achieve versus quality improvements gained. Make decisions on what is required given the time it will take to render it all out and what other demands are on the farm at that point.

Make sure you get as many elements to the compositors as early as possible. It does not necessarily have to be the signed off version, works in progress are useful as the compositor can start to build their comp script up and have the general layout of it signed off. When the final elements are available it will be a reasonably straight forward task of substituting these approved elements in and rendering.

Facilitate

The nature of the pipeline means your artists will always be needing inputs from other departments. Scheduling and estimating will provide a framework to departments to pass information to one another, do not rely on the schedule to deliver the assets between departments. Go in and find out how every team is progressing, whether they have everything they need and when they expect to output to the next team. Do this for every team so you can identify any potential delays and impediments.

Seek not to apportion blame to teams that are behind schedule. This will not actually resolve any issues and will only serve to add pressure to a particular team. The very nature of artists is that they always wants to present final polished work and rightly show a great deal of pride in their work. The nature of evolving software means that there is a constant learning curve for artists to go through. These technical constraints should not be overlooked. Often artists are under pressure to be completely up to date with the software packages, try to understand why they are falling behind and look to identify and address the issues as they occur. By being a facilitator rather than a harsh enforcer of the schedule as well as getting the artists to trust you will ultimately have them flag potential impediments earlier in the process while there is time to address them.

Often it will be the case of finding someone else who does know how to achieve a particular result or solve an issue that will allow the artist to carry on with their workflow and minimise the impact of these impediments. There will always be impediments to the workflow, it is the nature of the business that animation and effects teams are trying to surpass what was achieved last time or to break new ground. Software plays catch up to demands made of it. Do not pass on any additional stress to the artists, they are the ones who will complete the tasks, do whatever you can to facilitate them in finding a solution or work around.

Be flexible

This is the polar opposite of the producer who wields a heavy sword and enslaves the whole production to a schedule. Rather than being a weakness, being flexible is a great strength. Many producers cower away from having to change the schedule. Understandably no one is proud to admit mistakes. It may be the case that when your show starts slipping behind its schedule, it will be perceived as a failure on your behalf. Seeking out individuals to blame is not going to bring the show back on schedule. While some producers do this, ultimately it is self-defeating. Many shows will have to go off the rails and many people can blamed before a bad producer is found out.

Whatever the reasons behind this are, the only way out is by being flexible and compromising with your team to find solutions. Be prepared to update and re-plan as required, you will have to cut your cloth accordingly as you are committed to meeting a delivery date. Assess which sequences are ready for delivery, either early or on time and agree to adjust the order of the deliveries with your client. By providing other elements on time or early may give you some leeway for the problematic parts of the show. Also as people and resource become available from the delivered portions they can be reassigned to help the struggling sequences/teams.

Avoid being the producer who turns up to artists desks demanding that elements are delivered immediately. This accomplishes nothing and it *does not* make you look authoritative.

Contingency

If it can go wrong it probably will and when computers are involved the probability of things going wrong are significantly higher. Every production tends to discover one unknown software bug that will delay delivery of an asset. Much time is spent finding solutions to unknown problems, expect it. As mentioned earlier you are working in a constantly evolving arena, by definition you are doing things have not been done yet or doing things better than what was done before. Even if you are trying to recreate something done elsewhere consider that you do not have the same infrastructure and experience that another team had. Also you do not know what another team went through to realise the solution.

Building in contingency time to your schedule will take the pressure off your artists. Having artists under pressure, both time and performance pressure will adversely affect the quality of their work and their ability to hit deadlines. Whether or not you choose to make it known that contingency time is available will be down to how well you think your team will respond to it. But making sure that time and resources are available is a very prudent thing to do.

Listen and learn – the artist knows best

You are the producer, let the artist be the artist. You have hired them because they have a unique skillset that you do not possess - listen to them, have them involved as much as you can with scheduling, ask them to identify impediments and risks to achieving a delivery. Work with them to achieve the best order of things to deliver and what will need more contributions from downstream departments and how many upstream departments will be dependent upon their outputs.

Make an effort to know your artists and do not be so dependent upon the Head of Department (HoD). Hierarchies do have some positive points but being totally dependent upon one person to filter all the information to you will not allow you to see the whole picture.

As you know by now the business of CG and VFX is a highly technical one fraught with dependencies and inherent risk involved whenever trying something new and unproved. Naturally the HoD is the go to person, but the larger the teams involved the more complex the inner workings are of that team. You as a producer will be well served to acknowledge this and get to know the artists and ask them first hand what their concerns are and what potential impediments, risks and dependencies exist. You may be surprised to learn new issues that the HoD may not bring/has not yet brought to your attention.

When schedules start slipping, go and talk to your artists and ask them if the remaining items have been underbid and whether more time or resources are needed to catch up and ultimately deliver on time. It may not necessarily be a case of underbidding, there may have been a technical issue that they had to overcome and now they have overcome it the remaining jobs may run smoother. Once the schedule has slipped a knock on effect will impact on the downstream departments waiting for assets.

Not only will you get a more accurate estimate of the remaining tasks, but as a people management skill, when you have the artist tell you how much time they need to compete a task you will find that they are more likely to 'stick to' or even 'come in under' that bid when they were directly consulted. Having artists involved in the scheduling process gives them a stake in it far more than having schedules come from 'above'/being imposed upon them. It may turn out there was not too much variance in your estimates and theirs and potentially they may come in with faster turnarounds.

Do not be dependent upon one stream of information, especially the loudest stream.

Always check in - desk rounds

Dailies and shot management software will help you track the overall progress of the schedule but will not give you the granular detail that you require to make sure the right things are being developed/animated/simulated/lit according to the project's needs.

The problem with dailies is that you have blocked out a certain amount of the VFX supervisor's/director's time to see shots with a view to finalling them. No artist wants to show their work in progress to a cinema of people, much less the VFX supervisor/director to have it torn to shreds.

Artists are rightly very proud of their work and want to show it off in its most polished state. The problem with that is that *it takes a long time to get it to that final polished state*. The subjective nature of effects and animation mean that one person's interpretation of a brief can be quite different to another's. Having an artist go off for weeks to develop something that was not expected is a huge loss of time and effort on their and your behalf. It does not necessarily mean that it is wrong or bad, it is just not what was expected. Having lots of reference is one way to minimise this risk, you should always make sure reference is available at the briefing (obviously make sure every artists has a briefing – yes you will be surprised to find out this does not happen).

The best way to track the artist's work is to have daily desk rounds. This is quite different to dailies. The aim here is not to present final work, but more a progression of work. The VFX supervisor/director can then give feedback at an early stage and make sure the element is progressing in the way they want. Then by the time it is ready to be shown at dailies it has already had a lot of direction given to it that it should be approved quicker.

Be sure to manage expectations in these desk rounds. The trouble with animation, effects or any art discipline is that the first time you do it, it is not very good and does not resemble anything. The initial pass is a broad stroke outline which then gets iterated on to create what the artist feels comfortable showing. Having both parties know this at the outset that they are seeing initial states and works in progress will help the VFX supervisor/director have a two way dialogue with the artist.

It may well be that the VFX supervisor/director does not know what he/she wants yet. By seeing an initial animation something they can then give feedback. Having a first pass to give feedback on is better than a blank screen, where no one knows what they want and consequently wasting time sending the artist off in the wrong direction because of that.

There is a famous story of a theatre director who holds his head in his hands with a group of actors not knowing how to progress the scene. The producer walks past and asks what the problem is. The director says 'I don't know what to do'. The producer says 'well do something so we can change it'. When no one really knows what that final solution should be, having something on screen to show is the fastest way to get to the correct solution.

Be sure to keep these dailies involving as few people as possible and only include the artist, the ultimate decision maker (i.e. the VFX supervisor/director – as they will sign it off), HoD (as they will need to know who in their team needs to do what and can make recommendations on the best way to achieve it) and a coordinator to keep track of the progress and feedback into the schedule. Avoid making this design by committee at this stage, dailies is the place for group discussions. Desk rounds should make the artist feel comfortable to explore and share their ideas in a safe environment with the decision maker.

Conflict resolution

Do not underestimate this and how much time you will have to dedicate to this. Generally CG and VFX artists and TDs are an amiable bunch of people and left alone to get on with it, will work together to achieve a particular goal. When deadlines are being missed and pressure is mounting in any work environment, much less one that is so pipelined and dependency heavy you will see blame being readily apportioned. Beware of those who are constantly blaming others, *the ones making the most noise often contribute the least.*

The very nature of CG and VFX artists are that they will toil away solving technical issues and are more adept at communicating with computers and reading user guides than they are at standing up for themselves when someone is pouring scorn over them.

When you are rapidly approaching a deadline finding solutions is better than blaming people. Prevention is better than cure. Ultimately if you follow the guidelines outlined above you should avoid these situations occurring. Avoid apportioning any blame, especially in the heat of a pending crisis when you do not have the full facts. Look at your schedule and understand that it is 'impossible for one person to bring the whole show to its knees'.

One person may be responsible for a set of elements, if those elements are consistently being delivered late or under quality, identify why. Do not be too quick to dismiss the artist over it, there are many other factors to look at, perhaps the team dynamic is wrong, perhaps the schedule was too ambitious. Establish whether the tasks given fit their skillset – there is no point in giving a modelling and UV layout task to an effects artists and vice versa. As the producer make sure you know what peoples' skillsets are. Remember artists being very keen to please and show they are flexible and able to meet any challenge, will struggle and toil away before flagging any issues. It is your job to make sure you are scheduling the right type of work for any individual artist.

Check that the tools they have are fit for purpose. No two shots, even those that use the same effects rig will behave the same. A particular effect rig, for example a fluid simulation rig, may work when the camera is far away, but will not be suitable for when the camera is right in the centre of the effect as the fluid box will need a much higher resolution and cause huge increases in simulation time.

Also towards the end of the project there will be a scramble for resources, especially the render farm. At this stage of the project everyone's shot is a priority and you will have to handle the *farm politics* that we spoke about in part one.

Thou shalt share not hide the schedule - share and share alike

Make sure you share information especially as it pertains to the schedule to the whole team. The earlier you can share the information the better as a) the teams will be able to mange their workload when they know when the delivery is and b) any problematic deliveries can be flagged sooner. It is surprising how many producers do not like to share any such information - quite why some producers do not share information, you would need to ask them. Sometimes it may be out of not wanting to panic the production teams or not wanting to justify their decisions to a team of artists who *do not understand* how scheduling and production work. Whatever the reason is, it is a self defeating strategy as ultimately it will be the artists who deliver the show. By now you should know that it is better to work with artists in a relationship of equals, not to dictate from above because you are 'the producer'.

Listen to those around you - even if you do not like what they are saying

Sometimes you as the producer will make mistakes and be told you are wrong. Nobody really likes this when it happens, but to understand why you are wrong about a certain item is more important than any loss of face. The artists are dealing with a highly technical software pipeline which is always under constant stress from creative and technical demands. What was not an issue yesterday is an issue today, what was resolved last week is now an issue again today. Even the most stable of pipelines will to some extent always be in a state of perpetual flux. IT, infrastructure, R&D and Technical Directors will always be trying to maintain stability but when so many people are implementing features for the artist's needs there will be issues that need to be resolved. Do not assume to understand the issues that they are going through and expect it to be resolved simply, often one solution will favour one group of people ahead of others. Listen to all parties as they will have different perspectives on a proposed solution. Avoid being an arbitrator in these situations, instead aim to be a facilitator and work to solutions that will allow for the best compromise between the various stakeholders.

Do not adhere rigidly to a plan that is clearly failing - the schedule is your flexible friend

You have spent time budgeting, deliberating, consulting, you have double checked all your calculations, you have done complete due diligence in preparing the schedule and project plan, everything is correct but yet the schedule quickly falls behind and out of control. As much as you think others are to blame, when this happens, though, people are going to look to you as the producer and wonder how your plan is so far off. No amount of finger pointing at certain teams (even if it is justified) will mask the fact that you as a producer did not either see this risk, or worse still did not allow for any contingency.

There are two options open to you, you can either admit mistakes were made and start changing the schedule or bullheadedly plough through, thinking that it is a sign of weakness to change the precise plan you made, thinking it a sign of weakness and an admission of culpability. The reality is that you have a show to deliver by a deadline. You can either choose to make that delivery by adjusting workflows and changing the schedule you have built or you can start preparing your defence when the delivery is missed. This will depend upon you - whether you choose to address uncomfortable issues or to find others to blame. Ultimately you are the producer and will carry the can if the project should ever fail. There will be a lot of pressure from you from above, your boss will want to know why the delivery was missed, the bigger the miss, the more questions you will have to answer. You being solely responsible in this meeting will not have the whole CG team in the office with you. Depending upon how informed the boss is about the situation, you will choose to either present a factual account of the challenges involved and how you set about to address those or will start pointing the finger and naming scapegoats.

Whichever option you choose, the client will blame ultimately you, the boss will ultimately blame you, therefore it is better to try and rectify and redeem the situation as best as you can. Then regardless of the outcome - and if you try to rescue the situation (ahead of finding others to blame) the delivery will be successful - the boss and the client will see that you made every effort to reschedule and deliver the project rather than sticking to a plan that was flawed. Changing the schedule is not a sign of reactionary weakness and doubt, it is actually shows you are responsive and can adapt to changing circumstances.

Avoid nodding and grinning (inanely) when you do not understand what is going on

If you do not understand what someone says in a meeting just ask. Again it is not a sign of weakness or incompetence that you do not understand what a highly technical person is talking about. In reality technology and software advances are such that some of their peers do not understand what they are talking about. Just ask them what they mean in simple terms, this will benefit everyone as certain terms can be ambiguous and will help clarify the situation, especially when you have to communicate it to other teams, or when other teams are basing decisions on a different set of assumptions.

Check in - everyday if you are smart

Go around and have informal check ins with teams, keep your door open for people to check in with you. Encourage it, you do not necessarily have to log every single item, but keeping information flowing in two directions will allow risks which were not accounted for in the schedule to be identified sooner. Use this informal system in concert with a more formalised rigid structure which you keep to routinely. These informal conversations will help pre-empt any formal discussion further on. You cannot see every issue that will occur, no one can, part of your role as a producer is to pre-empt any issues that occur.

In closing

As you know now, the world of VFX and animation is always changing, the tools and technology that we use will have new names and functions, artists may not all be physically based in the same building, the outputs that you are working to will continuously evolve. One thing that will remain constant is the need to bring teams together and have them work towards a deadline. Your role as producer is critical in this, the old model of the producer laying down the rules to the team have gone. The team now is so specialised that different departments within the CG team are not able to keep abreast of the latest advances in the other teams. You as a producer who is looking after so many specialist teams will find it very difficult to be an authority on all the advances.

The best producers whilst still being planners are also facilitators. In truth that was a big unwritten part of the producer's role which made so many of them successful. By being a facilitator to many disparate teams who all need to work together will make sure that assets can be passed through the pipeline a lot more efficiently. In understanding this you can ensure that there is a constant flow of work that is evenly distributed across the whole of the pipeline and keep the project moving towards its successful delivery.

In closing I will leave you with Ten Golden Rules from VFX Producer Nathan Eyers.

The Ten Golden Rules by Nathan Eyers

1.   Relax

Easier said than done, but worth the investment I can assure you. Any production will have its challenges and risks, and from time to time things will scale out of your control, but this is when you need to keep your head. If you stay calm and composed then the best route forward will be much clearer.   Plus your team, your client, and your employer, will have confidence in you. Take yourself in to a quiet room to make this happen.

2.   Build strong relationships

A successful producer needs a good team working for and with them, so invest time in getting to know people, and what they are capable of doing, whether it's enriching a shot, or solving a technical problem they may have the solution. Extend your network of contacts outside the day to day, and get to know suppliers, external agencies, post-production houses, render farms, and freelancers.

3.   Plan and structure

Most projects kick-off at short notice, and you're often thrown in at the deep end, so buy yourself some time even if it's just a day to look at what lies ahead. You'll no doubt have your own systems for organising the project, but my advice is always to work backwards from the deadline.

4.   Interdependencies

Having read this book you'll know that one department relies upon another, and it's your job to identify and remove any blockages. Experience will help you spot the roadblocks a mile off, but in the early days you should learn from those around you.

5. Communicate

You should always be in listening mode. Find out how your clients, and team prefer to work. Hold daily meetings with the key members of the project. Get into the habit of doing this from the start and try not to let them slip. Use this to identify any warning signs, and as a basis for finding solutions.

6. Flexibility

Despite all your careful planning, there are so many variables that things will inevitably go wrong occasionally. It can't be avoided. The trick to limiting the damage is not to expose the production to too much risk. Factor in contingency from the start, and that means leaving a healthy percentage in the budget, allowing breathing space in and around the key milestones and deliverables, and lining up your artists and team members well in advance.

7. Resolving conflict

Often you'll be working with a highly skilled group of artists, and your job is to encourage a team ethic, and relaxed working environment. With tight deadlines, and long working hours, people's weaknesses can start to show. Look out for disagreements and put them to bed quickly. Flexing your negotiation skills is important, and so is showing leadership around decision-making.

8. References

Pull together a mood board, and provide references. It's one of the oldest and easiest tricks in the book, and it works. There's no need to leave the team guessing, nor the client for that matter. Bringing together clips, images, footage, and audio, will help with inspiration and clear direction, and if you want to develop the team spirit further, ask the artists to provide their own, and work them in to daily or weekly catch-ups.

9. Environment

Get the best technology, networks, servers, software licences, and kit that you can afford within your budget. Never expect to get by on the minimum. If you do you'll end up with frustrated artists, costly downtime, missed deliveries, and poor quality outputs. That's not to say that you should blow the budget, but do start as you mean to go on, and I guarantee that it will save you a lot of time and heartache in the long run.

10. Pizzas

Never expect your team to do something that you're not prepared to do yourself. That means if there's overtime, and weekends to be worked then you should expect to stick around too. You're in it together and that's what counts. OK so you might not be much use on the production side, but you can get the beers, order the pizzas, and keep everyone well nourished. Believe me it's the least that you can do, and they'll love you for it.

www.digitopiafilm.com

2

2D · 25, 33, 49, 50, 60, 71, 76, 85
2D compositing · 50

3

3D · 24, 26, 32, 35, 49, 50, 51, 59, 60, 61, 71, 74, 76, 85, 86, 87
3ds Max · 71

A

agents · 45, 46, 47
AGILE · 82
alpha · 52
ambiguous · 110
animatic · 23, 61, 62, 67
animatics · 23, 86
animation · 6, 16, 17, 20, 21, 23, 26, 29, 30, 31, 34, 35, 36, 39, 41, 42, 44, 47, 48, 49, 60, 61, 62, 63, 64, 67, 68, 69, 70, 73, 76, 78, 82, 85, 86, 88, 91, 97, 99, 100, 101, 102, 105, 106, 111
Animation · 6, 33, 34, 35, 46, 91
animations · 8, 31, 45, 46, 62, 63, 80, 87
animator · 30, 31, 35, 67, 68, 77, 91, 96, 98
animators · 23, 31, 35, 36, 43, 63, 67, 76, 77, 99

approved · 26, 30, 69, 70, 76, 78, 101, 106
arbitrator · 109
Art Department · 80
artists · 3, 8, 13, 15, 16, 17, 19, 31, 32, 33, 42, 43, 44, 52, 56, 63, 67, 69, 71, 72, 73, 76, 77, 79, 83, 86, 87, 88, 90, 91, 92, 95, 96, 97, 98, 99, 100, 102, 103, 104, 105, 107, 108, 111, 113, 114
asset · 12, 31, 32, 43, 63, 88, 103
assets · 17, 43, 63, 68, 69, 81, 99, 102, 104, 111
associate · 88
assumptions · 110
average · 57

B

backdrop · 37
background · 14, 35, 37, 73, 77
backgrounds · 76
backplate · 25, 26, 27, 44, 59, 60, 79
backplates · 44, 76
batch · 58
bats · 45, 46
beauty pass · 51
birds · 46
blade · 58, 59, 85
blades · 58, 59
blockages · 48, 70, 84, 112
blocked · 69, 83, 105
blood · 47
blue screen · 95
bones · 30

116

bottlenecks · 69, 101
branching · 31
budget · 6, 12, 13, 15, 16, 17, 20, 23, 35, 57, 63, 68, 70, 96, 97, 113, 114
budgeting · 63, 97, 109
bullet impacts · 39, 47
bump · 32
burndown chart · 88
business case · 57
business expenses · 66

C

cache · 45
caches · 45
cameras · 26, 63, 67, 68, 69, 77, 78, 95
cancelled · 69
capacity · 57, 59
CG · 2, 3, 4, 5, 6, 8, 13, 14, 15, 16, 22, 24, 30, 46, 59, 60, 75, 76, 77, 78, 79, 80, 94, 96, 101, 104, 107, 109, 111
CGI · 6, 13, 16, 21, 61, 75, 85
channels · 31, 76
Character · 43
client · 14, 15, 26, 56, 69, 70, 72, 78, 88, 91, 103, 110, 112, 113
client expectations · 15
cloth · 20, 41, 43, 45, 47, 57, 103
Cloth · 41
code · 33, 81, 82
colliding · 45
collision · 39, 45
colour · 19, 32, 60
colour palette · 19
Communicate · 99, 113

Communication · 72
composited · 37, 44, 60, 78, 79
composites · 37, 44
compositing · 44, 50, 59, 60, 62, 75, 78, 85, 89, 96
Compositing · 15, 59
compositor · 44, 50, 51, 59, 78, 91, 101
compromise · 26, 109
computers · 13, 63, 103, 107
concept art · 19, 20, 22, 61, 80, 93, 94, 95
Concept art · 19
Conflict · 107
conform · 62, 91
considerations · 13, 14, 17, 39, 49, 56, 58, 77, 81
contingency · 83, 103, 109, 113
Contingency · 103
control · 40, 43, 45, 50, 83, 86, 87, 109, 112
controls · 30, 31, 40, 43, 87
Controls · 43
coordinate system · 32
coordinator · 72, 88, 106
cores · 56, 58
cost · 23, 27, 35, 65, 66, 93, 94
criteria · 59
cross hairs · 76
crowd · 20, 44, 45, 46, 47, 48, 57, 77
crowd sim · 45, 46, 47
crowd simulation · 20, 44, 45, 46, 47, 48, 57
crunch · 61
cut · 69, 73, 103

117

D

dailies · 69, 72, 73, 88, 91, 99, 100, 105, 106
data · 27, 35, 36, 45, 48, 57, 95, 96
database · 68, 80
deadlines · 60, 70, 99, 101, 104, 107, 113
debris · 39
decision maker · 106
declaration · 80, 81
delivery · 49, 56, 57, 72, 73, 88, 90, 91, 103, 104, 108, 109, 111
delivery date · 49
department · 12, 17, 20, 25, 26, 31, 44, 45, 48, 49, 50, 57, 60, 63, 79, 80, 82, 83, 96, 99, 112
dependencies · 16, 17, 28, 30, 46, 47, 48, 57, 61, 62, 63, 70, 79, 83, 84, 87, 104
depth · 13, 32, 52, 77
design · 61, 62, 79, 80, 81, 82, 83, 87, 106
designers · 79, 81, 100
desk rounds · 88, 91, 100, 105, 106
Desk rounds · 106
destruction · 39
destructive · 31
development · 30, 60, 73, 88, 98
diffuse · 52
digital · 12, 15, 17, 20, 26, 37
digital matte painting · 20, 37
Digital Matte Painting · 9, 37
diminishing returns · 54, 97
direction · 32, 37, 88, 92, 99, 106, 113
dirt · 35, 39, 47

displacement · 32
distinct features · 25, 26, 27
distorted · 77
DMP · 20, 37, 38
downstream · 22, 26, 28, 30, 47, 48, 57, 59, 70, 78, 88, 104
downtime · 17, 114
Due dates · 69
duration · 23, 68
dust · 23, 39, 40, 47, 77, 79

E

edit · 62
editing · 23, 62
effect · 41, 43, 44, 45, 83, 97, 100, 104, 107
effects · 5, 6, 12, 13, 15, 19, 20, 21, 26, 35, 39, 40, 41, 42, 43, 45, 47, 48, 60, 61, 62, 71, 73, 74, 76, 77, 80, 81, 83, 85, 86, 93, 94, 96, 97, 99, 101, 102, 105, 106, 107
Effects · 3, 6, 12, 35, 39, 44, 47, 94
elements · 15, 20, 21, 23, 26, 37, 41, 42, 43, 44, 60, 65, 75, 76, 77, 79, 82, 84, 89, 94, 95, 96, 101, 103, 107
environment · 19, 20, 21, 25, 26, 37, 38, 39, 45, 47, 61, 76, 80, 106, 107, 113
environments · 19, 42, 62, 68
explosions · 39
exported · 26

F

facilitator · 102, 109, 111
facilitators · 111
facility · 15, 16, 36, 91, 95, 96, 97
fair usage policy · 59
farm · 44, 45, 52, 55, 56, 57, 58, 59, 70, 78, 82, 85, 101, 108
Farm · 57
fast · 26, 32, 40, 58, 88, 91, 92
feather · 41
feedback · 31, 44, 69, 73, 82, 88, 92, 97, 98, 99, 100, 105, 106
files · 58
final frame · 49
fire · 20, 21, 39, 41, 46, 47, 100
fish · 45, 46
flattening · 77
Flexibility · 113
flip booking · 70
flipbooking · 23
Fluid · 40
fluids · 40, 41
footage · 25, 75, 76, 78, 85, 113
foreground · 27, 37, 95
formatting · 62
frame lengths · 68
frame rate · 82
frames per second · 76, 82
freeware · 37
fur · 41, 42, 43, 91

G

games · 6, 8, 13, 15, 17, 40, 79, 80, 81, 82, 100
Gant chart · 70

gaseous · 40
generalist · 86
geometry · 24, 26, 39, 41, 45, 46
goodwill · 88, 97
grading · 44, 60
granular · 50, 105
graphics · 6, 79, 80
ground plane · 45, 46
GUI · 80

H

hair · 29, 41, 43, 45, 47, 57
hard surface · 28, 29, 32
HDRI · 9, 37, 38
hierarchy · 43, 88
High Dynamic Range Image · 37
Houdini · 15
hue · 50

I

ID · 52
idle states · 45
illumination · 52
images · 3, 5, 20, 22, 24, 38, 42, 50, 73, 76, 82, 89, 113
impediments · 83, 102, 104
in progress · 69, 101, 105, 106
infrastructure · 13, 71, 103, 108
input · 33, 34, 37, 70, 86
instanced · 41
Instancing · 39
Interdependencies · 112
iterating · 54, 97
iteration · 30, 54, 63, 66, 68

119

iterations · 50, 54, 66, 69, 72, 73, 94, 96, 97
iterative · 81

J

joints · 30
jpgs · 77

L

lay out · 32
levels · 26, 50
licences · 56, 57, 85, 114
light · 3, 33, 37, 38, 44, 81, 87, 91
lighter · 31, 37, 44, 49, 51, 91
lighting · 26, 33, 35, 37, 38, 42, 44, 45, 48, 49, 50, 54, 57, 58, 60, 62, 64, 66, 76, 77, 80, 85, 86, 87, 89, 91, 95, 99
Lighting · 9, 48, 49
lights · 44, 48
Linux · 71
live action · 39, 59, 75, 78
loading · 58
local machine · 54
look development · 33, 35, 37, 48, 50, 60, 63, 77, 101
Look Development · 33, 48

M

maps · 32, 80
Match moving · 24
matchmove · 25, 26, 76, 77, 95, 96
matchmover · 25, 27

matchmovers · 25, 26, 27, 76
matchmoves · 26
matchmoving · 25, 77, 78, 85
Matchmoving · 24, 77
Maya · 15, 71
memory · 76, 82, 97
meshing · 40
micromanage · 98
midground · 37
mid-ground · 27
milestone · 83
milestones · 62, 83, 87, 113
model · 19, 21, 29, 30, 31, 32, 33, 35, 43, 45, 61, 63, 69, 71, 86, 91, 111
modelled · 62, 82
modeller · 29, 33, 91
modellers · 28, 33
modelling · 23, 28, 29, 35, 39, 46, 47, 48, 63, 85, 86, 101, 107
Modelling · 9, 28, 29
models · 31, 32, 36, 42, 48, 63, 87, 91
motion capture · 34, 35, 45
Motion capture · 35
Multiple users · 55

N

nested · 43
nodal · 34
node · 34, 54, 57, 58
nodes · 33, 34, 55, 58
normal · 32, 52, 58
Nuke · 15, 71

120

O

Olympics · 6, 7, 18
on hold · 69
organic · 28, 29
overflow · 58

P

paint · 32, 33, 38, 95
parallel · 35, 63, 80
parameters · 43
Particle · 39
particles · 39, 40, 41
Passes · 9, 49
photographed · 38
physics · 41
pipeline · 3, 12, 13, 14, 17, 30, 31, 34, 45, 59, 60, 61, 63, 69, 71, 72, 73, 75, 78, 80, 86, 87, 101, 102, 108, 111
pipelines · 15, 35, 108
placeholder · 83
Plan · 93, 112
planners · 111
playback · 45, 73, 76, 82
playblast · 44, 70
playblasting · 23
playblasts · 70
politics · 57, 108
Politics · 57
pool · 58, 59
pooling · 58
pools · 56, 58
post production · 6, 15, 16, 17, 95
post-production · 8, 96, 112
Practicalities · 85

prep · 72, 76, 85
Preparing · 76
Preproduction · 61
previsualisation · 23
previz · 23, 31, 61, 63, 67, 86, 94, 97, 101
Previz · 23, 44, 62
priorities · 57, 101
prioritised · 79
probability · 103
producer · 6, 7, 12, 13, 14, 15, 16, 17, 20, 28, 31, 33, 35, 46, 47, 48, 49, 52, 55, 57, 59, 62, 63, 77, 79, 81, 82, 83, 87, 88, 92, 93, 99, 102, 103, 104, 106, 107, 108, 109, 110, 111, 112
production coordination · 88
programmers · 15, 79, 100
programming · 79, 80, 81, 82, 83
project management · 15, 70, 71, 73
Project Management · 72
project plan · 109
props · 35, 41, 42, 61, 68, 76, 81
proxy · 30
publishing · 63, 68

Q

QA · 79, 80, 82, 83, 84
Quality Assurance · 82, 83
queue · 58
queues · 58

R

R&D · 77, 108

121

VFX and CG Survival Guide for Filmmakers and Producers

rain · 20, 21, 39
rain effects · 20
Rain splashes · 47
reel · 82, 98
reference · 42, 44, 66, 95, 96, 105
Reference · 42, 44
References · 113
relight · 62
removal · 76
render · 20, 23, 24, 26, 40, 44, 45, 49, 50, 51, 52, 53, 54, 55, 56, 57, 58, 59, 62, 70, 77, 78, 82, 85, 87, 91, 101, 108, 112
render farm · 45, 57, 58, 59, 71
Render Farms · 52
rendered · 43, 44, 45, 50, 70, 75, 77, 78, 82, 89
rendering · 26, 33, 35, 44, 45, 48, 49, 50, 52, 53, 54, 56, 58, 59, 62, 64, 70, 76, 85, 91, 101
Rendering · 52
Renderman · 15
renders · 44, 49, 55, 57, 58, 59, 60, 63, 70, 101
reschedule · 82, 110
resolved · 84, 108
resources · 4, 56, 63, 71, 97, 101, 104, 108
review · 4, 5, 56, 69, 72, 73
Revolver · 8, 67, 71, 72, 73
rig · 30, 31, 35, 43, 45, 61, 62, 77, 88, 101, 107
rigging · 20, 29, 30, 31, 35, 63, 80, 85, 89
Rigging · 30
rigid body dynamics · 47
rigid body simulation · 39
Rigid body simulations · 41
risks · 83, 104, 110, 112

roto · 72, 76, 96
Roto · 76
rotoscoping · 76
running cycles · 45
RV · 73

S

sand · 27, 39
scapegoats · 110
scene · 3, 26, 48, 58, 60, 63, 96, 106
schedule · 16, 20, 21, 27, 30, 31, 62, 63, 68, 69, 77, 79, 82, 83, 88, 89, 90, 92, 97, 100, 102, 103, 104, 105, 106, 107, 108, 109, 110
schedules · 15, 87, 98, 104, 105
scheduling · 17, 26, 47, 49, 63, 67, 83, 104, 105, 107, 108
Scheduling · 61, 90, 102
scratches · 77
screening room · 73
script · 17, 23, 44, 50, 60, 61, 101
self critique · 98
sequence · 21, 23, 24, 31, 35, 44, 49, 50, 53, 55, 56, 58, 59, 62, 64, 66, 67, 70, 76, 90, 92, 99
sequences · 6, 15, 21, 46, 49, 55, 60, 64, 67, 70, 99, 103
Set extensions · 96
shaders · 33, 63
shading · 30, 33, 34, 35, 61, 63
Shading · 33
shot · 12, 15, 17, 18, 19, 21, 24, 25, 26, 27, 31, 41, 42, 44, 48, 49, 52, 63, 64, 67, 68, 69, 70, 72, 73, 77, 82, 85, 86, 88, 90,

122

92, 93, 94, 96, 97, 99, 100, 105, 108, 112
shot management · 68, 70, 85, 99, 105
Shot names · 68
Shot status · 69
Shotgun · 8, 67, 71, 72, 73, 74
shots · 14, 15, 17, 19, 20, 21, 23, 25, 26, 27, 30, 31, 35, 37, 41, 43, 47, 49, 50, 52, 61, 62, 63, 64, 67, 68, 69, 70, 71, 72, 78, 86, 90, 95, 96, 97, 98, 99, 100, 105, 107
show · 13, 15, 16, 17, 28, 32, 41, 49, 54, 57, 59, 70, 72, 85, 86, 87, 88, 90, 94, 99, 102, 103, 105, 106, 107, 108, 109, 113
showreels · 17, 98
signed off · 26, 27, 30, 44, 79, 101
simulation · 39, 40, 41, 44, 45, 48, 76, 86, 87, 107
simultaneously · 57
skeleton · 30
Skills · 15
skillset · 60, 104, 107
skillsets · 19, 59, 107
skinning · 30
skyscapes · 37
slap comping · 44
slow · 58, 83, 100
smoke · 21, 23, 39, 41, 79, 96
snow · 27, 39, 40
software · 15, 17, 25, 26, 27, 28, 33, 40, 41, 56, 57, 58, 63, 66, 68, 70, 72, 74, 76, 85, 86, 87, 99, 102, 103, 105, 108, 110, 114
solution · 25, 27, 59, 96, 101, 102, 103, 106, 109, 112

solve · 25, 26, 27, 102
solved · 26
sound · 13, 60, 62, 81
specialist · 37, 59, 67, 87, 111
specular · 52
spreadsheet · 67, 70
SPRINT · 82
sprites · 40
static geometry · 26
status · 70, 80, 99, 100
stereo · 18, 71, 72, 74
stitched · 38
stock libraries · 37
story boarding · 19
storyboard · 21, 61
storyboards · 23
Structure · 101
subscription · 37
substituted · 30, 39
supervisor · 27, 30, 44, 69, 70, 72, 73, 88, 91, 95, 96, 99, 100, 105, 106
surface · 29, 32, 33, 62, 81
surfacers · 33

T

task · 14, 25, 52, 63, 70, 78, 83, 86, 87, 101, 105, 107
TD · 41, 42, 43, 45
Technical Director · 42
Technical Directors · 15, 108
texture · 29, 32, 33, 87
Texture · 32
textures · 32, 33, 40, 44, 63, 96
texturing · 30, 32, 33, 35, 44, 61, 63, 85, 95, 101
Texturing · 32, 35

track · 25, 26, 27, 72, 95, 101, 105, 106
tracking · 25, 27, 72, 73, 85, 92, 95, 96
tracking markers · 25, 95

U

underbidding · 104
unwrapped · 32
UV layout · 32, 33, 85, 86, 107
UVs · 29, 32, 86

V

vector · 52
vehicles · 35
VFX · 2, 3, 4, 5, 6, 7, 8, 12, 13, 14, 15, 16, 17, 22, 30, 31, 34, 44, 59, 67, 68, 70, 71, 72, 73, 75, 76, 85, 87, 88, 91, 93, 94, 95, 96, 98, 99, 100, 101, 104, 105, 106, 107, 111

videos · 42
virtual camera · 23, 24, 25, 26, 77, 95

W

waiting · 59, 91, 104
water · 21, 39, 42, 47, 86
weapon · 47
web conferencing · 100
wires · 76
workflow · 3, 72, 73, 82, 101, 102
workflows · 16, 98, 109
workgroups · 56
workload · 83, 108
workspace · 32
workspaces · 60

X

XY · 32

124

Printed in Great Britain
by Amazon.co.uk, Ltd.,
Marston Gate.